Praise for *Our Character at Work*

"There's lots of information floating around in our world about leadership and work. But wisdom is harder to come by. *Our Character at Work* is in the wisdom business."

John Ortberg, Senior Pastor of Menlo Park
Presbyterian Church and author of *All the Places to Go*

"*Our Character at Work* is insightful, inspiring, and a must-read for those who desire to be effective leaders in the twenty-first century. Hunter has created a leadership classic!"

Foley Beach, Archbishop and Primate
Anglican Church in North America

"The most difficult aspect of servant leadership is the personal journey to form and maintain a servant's heart. Todd Hunter shares generously from his observations and experiences to help us forge a deeper conviction and commitment to serving others, as the path to better performance and a better work-place. Take in his teaching. It will stretch your soul."

Cheryl A. Bachelder, CEO, Popeyes Louisiana
Kitchen, Inc., Author of *Dare to Serve: How to Drive Superior
Results by Serving Others*

"Bishop Todd Hunter has dedicated his life to the most significant mission on the planet—waking humanity up to its fullest potential. With an understandable and compelling framework to chew on, and actionable steps to dive into, *Our Character at Work* is a must-read for anyone who seeks significance and impact. He proves that all of life works better when we give ourselves away for the sake of others. May our Boomers and

X'ers humbly align to his vision, and may our Millennials learn out of the gate that this is THE WAY to do things at work."

Scott Schimmel, President and Chief Guide of YouSchool

"I don't much like books on leadership. Too much 1, 2, 3, etc. for me. But Todd Hunter's book on leadership is different because it is really about spiritual formation and how servant leadership emerges from a heart being shaped by Jesus. *Our Character at Work* is more like a quiet conversation with a wise and loving friend than an essay on management styles. Would that the leaders in our lives listen deeply to what he has to say. Would that we become this kind of leader."

Richard Peace, PhD, Robert Boyd Munger
Professor of Evangelism & Spiritual Formation at
Fuller Theological Seminary in Pasadena, California

"Too few leaders, and even fewer books on leadership, successfully connect moral character and courage with effectiveness. Thus we are too often left to wonder, both individually and corporately, how we are to develop, and where we can find skillful leaders who also possess integrity and strength. Fortunately, Todd Hunter knows precisely what kinds of leaders we require, and demonstrates how our world thrives under their guidance and suffers in their absence. Hunter helps us understand why servant leaders, in every area of our society, must be held to account for knowing what is right and have the courage to do the right thing. This book gives us a vision of what could be, right where we live and work. Todd calls for every leader to face the inner transformation necessary to become worthy of their calling to pursue the highest common good for the benefit of all concerned. Best of all, Todd reminds us at every turn that Jesus Christ sets the standard and shows the way."

Gary Black, Jr., PhD, Professor of Theology and
Coauthor of *The Divine Conspiracy Continued*

Our Character at Work

Success from the Heart of Servant Leadership

TODD D. HUNTER

Foreword by Art Barter

Our Character at Work: Success from the Heart of Servant Leadership

Published by Wheatmark
1760 East River Road, Suite 145
Tucson, Arizona 85718 USA
www.wheatmark.com

ISBN: 978-1-62787-291-1 (paperback)
ISBN: 978-1-62797-293-5 (hardcover)
ISBN: 978-1-62787-292-8 (ebook)
LCCN: 2015942206

ISBN 978-0-8308-4427-2 (print)
ISBN 978-0-8308-9861-9 (digital)

For brothers and servant leaders
Corporal Dennis Wayne Hunter, who laid down his life,
and
Chief Craig Allen Hunter, who put his life on the line

"Greater love has no one than this:
to lay down one's life for one's friends."

Contents

Foreword

As I travel around the country teaching others how to implement servant leadership, I am both encouraged and surprised about what I hear from leaders about their faith. Some are nervous about letting any part of their faith show and some are ready to conquer the world and save others, while most are struggling with this one question: Can I live my faith in the workplace? I've heard a lot of concerns about political correctness and legalities, but more often I hear a fear of being known as a leader of faith.

At an event I recently attended, I met two men of faith, one of whom talked about being a man of God for his family, leading at home under God's principles. He talked about how his family sees a difference in him and their willingness to follow a husband or father of faith. The other man is a Chief Operating Officer (COO) in a company where his boss is the CEO and not a man of faith. The COO expressed a desire to lead as a servant leader, but at the same time hesitated to fully engage his faith at work. As we talked, he said he is encouraged to meet leaders who are leading with their faith seven days a week. He stated, "we need more men like you Art, willing to be servant leaders in the marketplace." I was quick to point out there are a lot of servant leaders living their faith in companies today.

The conversation then turned to sharing our faith. The first gentleman asked, "Where do we share our faith with others first? Is it in our home, our extended family or our community?" I am always amazed that Christians believe that everyone needs to be an evangelist through their presence with others and their words. Many do not understand their faith starts with their character through their behaviors, showing others what it means to be a leader of faith. When Jesus was asked which of the commandments is most important, he replied, "Love the Lord your God with all your heart and with all your soul and with all your mind and with all your strength. The second is this, love your neighbor as yourself. There is no greater commandment than these." (Mark 12: 30-31). Both commandments are based on behaviors.

In the lobby of our company, the following sign greets all our visitors:

In God We Trust
   In People We Invest

That was not always on our wall. You see, I was trained in the power model in the corporate world, focused on short-term results without too much care for what it took to get them. While a power leader, I had the following on an 8.5 x 11 piece of paper on my wall behind my desk:

In God We Trust
   All Others Bring Data

In my power leadership days, it was all about proving to me that you were worth listening to, that you had data to convince me you were worth listening to. I can't recall a time when Jesus asked for data before he would listen to someone. I was not willing to invest my time with anyone unless they had data.

Transforming my thinking and behaviors didn't come easy. I was fortunate to meet Todd Hunter in 2005 and discover we had a common interest in servant leadership. My leadership transformation began in 2001 when I let God back in my life. In 2003, Ken Blanchard spoke at my church and asked if we really believed what we believe. The title of his talk that night was, "Lead Like Jesus, It's a Mandate." He taught us, and challenged us, that if we wanted to be obedient in our faith we had no other choice than to lead like Jesus, to be a servant leader. Over the years, Ken has helped me understand what it means to really believe what you believe.

When we first bought Datron World Communications, Inc., we expressed our faith by putting *In God We Trust* on the lobby wall. Still fresh in my renewed faith, I had yet to discover that my behaviors were more powerful than words. With the help of my pastor, along with Todd and other Christian leaders, I came to realize that trusting God only reflects one of the two most important commandments. We needed to add, *In People We Invest* to reflect the second commandment to treat others like ourselves. Transforming my own faith through my behaviors is a lifelong journey. When I am challenged in this area of my life, I am thankful for the grace God provides us anew each and every morning.

What I've learned over the past ten years in running our company under godly principles is that living your faith is all about your behaviors. We can influence more people by our behaviors than we can with our words. What I love about Todd is that he teaches the transformation of your heart with a focus toward implementing your faith, not just learning about it. In this book, he has provided scripture for study to help you transform your heart and mind, but more importantly how to live or implement your faith 24/7, reinforced by actual stories of where others have lived life for the sake of others, just as Jesus did.

I encourage you to live your faith, each and every day, through your behaviors. *Our Character at Work* will define who you are in your faith and help you influence others through your behavior. I believe the true measure of yourself as a servant leader is the stories of those you have influenced through your behaviors. In the end, it is your behaviors that will provide you the opportunity to share your faith with the person God puts in front of you at the time needed to reach that heart.

On this journey with you.

Under the Same Wings,
Art Barter
President and CEO
Datron World Communications, Inc.

President and CEO
Servant Leadership Institute, Inc.

Introduction

Beginning the Journey of
Servant Leadership

> At the moment we see some-
> thing beautiful we undergo a
> radical decentering. Beauty, ac-
> cording to Weil, requires us "to
> give up our imaginary position
> as the center. . . . A transforma-
> tion then takes place at the very
> roots of our sensibility."
>
> Elaine Scarry, *On Beauty*
> *and Being Just*

My boss sucks. The deep discouragement from which bitter words like those flow is the number one reason people hate and disconnect from their jobs.[1] These disgruntled employees may stay in the building—they will undoubtedly continue to cash their paychecks—but their hearts, minds, and focus will be else-where. Bitterness toward leaders in the workplace distracts workers from doing good work or putting in a fair day of work for a fair wage. To be alive is to pay attention to something. The question is: on what *will* workers focus? Will it be the value they can bring to their work, or their growing angst, cynicism, and sullen resentment toward management?

The toll on our economy from employee disengagement is larger than any of us can imagine. Disgruntled employees cause retail prices to rise. The relational toll is even worse: human trust sinks. Contempt or hatred for others eats away at and ultimately destroys one's soul. Imagine the deep frustration employees bring home every evening. Crossing the threshold from the porch to the entryway, frustration too often results in cutting remarks to one's spouse. Depression and hopelessness cause people to check out, not just from their work but also from their child's homework. Medicating workplace-based pain with food, drugs, alcohol, or various web-based obsessions and addictions keep an army of therapists and ER doctors employed.

The world is troubled in many ways, and people want to help. Social justice issues are popular. You know: "Save the Rain Forest" or "Free the Whales." I get the impulse. But my cause, my contribution to humankind, is *servant leadership*. I'm troubled by visions of a depressed workforce with slumped shoulders, tight necks, anxiety-driven headaches, and family relationships torn asunder by angry outbursts.

My heart sings at the thought of a fairly treated, contented, and appropriately challenged workforce that experiences personal and professional growth on the job. *My goal is to reduce the systemic harm that happens to hundreds of millions of workers every day at the hand of poor leaders.*

The best way to do this is to create thousands of new servant leaders.

Max De Pree, the highly respected CEO of Herman Miller Inc. tells us organizations have to have *a moral purpose.* "Without moral purpose, competence has no measure, and trust has no goal. Moral purpose is kept aflame by the sense of giving an account to a higher being."[2] In this book I will discuss the importance of one's worldview—a certain way of thinking and being in the world, a certain way of carrying oneself—that leads to a moral purpose inherent in the practice of servant leadership. The nature of servant leadership comes to us from our Maker, who reminds us to love others in the pursuit of good for everyone who crosses our path: employee, supplier, outside contractor, or client.

This book will reveal how to get at and work with the most important factors of leadership: your heart, your inner person, the current structure of your desires, beliefs, and attitudes. This book will foster changes in your leadership style that you previously thought impossible.

Is There a Model We Can Imitate?

Perhaps you picked up this book because you have seen the dreadful harm of self-centered leadership. Maybe you desire to be more patient, kind, and humane. To produce such leaders we need a model, a teacher. In this book, I look to Jesus as our paradigm: his life, his manner of being in the world, his example of servant leadership. I cannot find a better model, a more powerful example, and a more insightful teacher than Jesus. If you can find a better model than Jesus, you should emulate that person. Jesus wouldn't mind; he has nothing left to prove. But I doubt such a person exists. Whether you are a Christian or not even religious, it is not controversial to say that Jesus is the towering person of human history.

As you read and learn, begin to gently, quietly, and unobtrusively put Jesus's words into practice. Don't allow yourself to think, *I can't do what Jesus did; he was divine!* He taught that we could learn to do what he did, and speak as he spoke. We can't have it both ways: either he knew what he was talking about or he didn't. Are you willing to take Jesus as your teacher in servant leadership?

I encourage you to go on the journey of inner transformation so the life you see in Jesus begins to flow naturally from you. As this growth begins, observe what happens in the people you lead. Goodness and productivity will emerge, which has the potential to revolutionize the workplace.

The case for servant leadership being good for the bottom line is made elsewhere.[3] So too are best practices for implementing servant leadership. This book takes its place in the literature of servant leadership by going beyond income statements and balance sheets, beyond mere human resource issues, to the heart of the woman or man who seeks to become or improve as a servant leader.

My observation of servant-led organizations and my own experience leads me to believe that Max De Pree is spot on: "Good numbers don't result from managing numbers."[4] Good numbers come from a corporate culture in which people thrive by participating in doing good work made meaningful under the stewardship of a servant leader.[5]

Leadership Malpractice

Throughout this book we'll look into the thinking processes of servant leadership. I'll share some anecdotes that identify the malpractice of "positional" or "power" leadership. I share these negative examples for educational purposes only, knowing that it is never fair to judge a leader's career based on a few bad moments or loose comments.

As I make the case for servant leadership, we must face these facts: across the world, incidents of harmful leadership in the workplace add up to millions per day, scores of millions a month and hundreds of millions a year. Such mismanagement affects real human beings—our neighbors and families—fostering discouragement, defeat, and disengagement at work. According to a recent report in the *Washington Post*, "The US labor force is still shrinking rapidly. Back in 2007, 66 percent of Americans had a job or were actively seeking work. Today, that number is at 62.8 percent—the lowest level since 1977."[6] While there are obvious cyclical economic reasons that underlie this, my observations lead me to conclude that one contributing factor is the horrible experience people have at work. Low wages are tough to take. Part-time hours, odd shifts, and no benefits don't boost morale. But add to that bad leadership, and, well, millions drop out.

I have witnessed the destructive effect of bad leadership firsthand in my own family. As a teenager, thrilled to have his first job in retail as a stock clerk and eager to please, my son got up every morning at four to be at work on time at five. He never missed and was never late. But his leaders routinely showed up late, unlocked the store doors late, and then berated the young staff for not being done with their stock work when the store opened. These leaders were frustrated with their district managers and took out their frustration on the young staff. They gave the staff jobs with no context, little training, and no help.[7]

Leaving that job a little hurt and significantly disillusioned about leaders, my son got a new job at local café. Here, the kitchen boss did not do his job. He often left without explanation for hours at a time to go home and smoke marijuana. Many times he would do the same behind the building before opening. The boss was so often late to open the café that my son got a key so he could do it. The kitchen boss refused to pitch in during customer rushes, throwing the whole day off and making good service impossible. My son was actually running the kitchen. In a classic instance of positional/power leadership, the boss asked my son to order four cases of lettuce for the busy weekend crowds. My son knew they only needed two and that the general manager would be mad at the wasted food on Monday morning. But his leader said, "I'm the manager—just order it." As predicted it was too much lettuce and the GM complained.

Trying to find a peaceful place to work by moving to another restaurant, my son found that the general manager was a friend of the owner and that the owner was enabling the general manager's alcoholism. Always angry about something and unreasonable about most things, this leader never pitched in to help, consistently misjudged employees, and was notorious for yelling while poking employees in the chest.

"Well," you may protest, "retail and restaurants are notorious places to work, with their crazy pace, the never-ending stress, and the constant emotional scenes acted out by leaders and their staff." That may be true, but it seems to me that under the pressure of the rising costs of goods, demands for higher pay, poorly performing vendors, and shrinking margins on sales, most sectors of the workplace are catching up with retail and food service as tough places to work.

At the gym this morning I heard for the umpteenth time

the enduring tune "Imagine," written by and performed by John Lennon. I'm sure you too can recall these bits of it: "Imagine all the people living life in peace. . . . It's easy if you try. . . . You may say I'm a dreamer." "Well John," I want to say, "given today's realities, I actually *can't* imagine all the people in the workplace living life in peace. Nothing in the forty-plus years since you wrote the song would bring such confidence. I think you were a dreamer. But it was a great dream, and *I want to join you.*"

But the peace envisioned in the song is not "easy if you try." In fact it is impossible if you simply *try*. The only hope is to be *transformed*. That is the core vision of this book, the transformation of leaders who, for instance, show up on time as an act of service to the young people they lead, who show them the ropes as a act of neighborly love, who serve their employees rather than use them as cover for their drug use, and who patiently teach rather scream and yell.

A Guidebook and a Coach

In athletics I was always in the starting lineup. But I was never *the star*. I had the joy of playing with guys who were stars. Guys who made it to the big leagues. In some cases, guys who made it to the hall of fame.

Star athletes, however, rarely make good coaches. However, average guys like me, who love the game and have the passion to teach it to others, often become good coaches. After two decades of learning to be a servant leader through trial and error, I have a passion for helping others become the kinds of people who can be servant leaders. In these pages I'll be your coach on the journey to transforming your heart into that of a servant leader.

I have been on this journey for twenty-three years. Working on my own inner stuff for the sake of leading others well has been fascinating, joyful, and deeply fulfilling. It can be for you too.

I spent twelve years as president of two multimillion dollar nonprofits, managing hundreds of employees and doing all the tasks the leader of any organization would do. I've also served as a pastor, a bishop, an author, a speaker, and a professor. I've made mistakes. I've discovered my weaknesses, as well as my strengths, in being a servant leader. These are the experiences I draw from for this book.

Like you, I've worked with diverse people in all their wonderful complexities. I love people and want them to experience my leadership for their good. I also love the enterprises I have led and want them to perform to their highest potential.

To do this, I have learned to take my cues from God. Before we go on, let me say a couple more words about God. First, you can benefit from this book without sharing my exact beliefs about God. Second, I want to assert that God knows about work, workplaces, and leadership. God worked. He led. According to the ancient text of Scripture, God created and produced "goods." Metaphorically, we could say that from his inner research and development staff, God created stuff, managing the process along the way to its completion. All was well until the pinnacle of his creation—humankind—decided to go their own rebellious way.

Then, Jesus came on the scene. He also worked. He led a world-changing movement bigger than the Enlightenment, the Industrial Revolution, or the Technological Revolution combined! The Jesus Revolution spread though Jesus's training of a few women and a dozen men. He was a master of human resource development.

Jesus motivated people by his selfless, Spirit-empowered leadership. With his small team, he faced down the ruthless Roman regime and the powerful religious leaders of his day. Jesus's followers brought to their brutally broken society a new way of being human. A new way to lead.

Servant leaders working with God never have to grab for power, strive for position, or harm others to get their way. Why? Because, when we work with God we are working in concert with ultimate power, influence, and capacity. When God shares his clout with us, we do not need to rob others of theirs. Rather, we are so rich in power, influence, and capacity that we can share it liberally with workmates, as appropriate in a given situation.

Servant leadership is connected to the two-thousand-years-long Jesus movement. It is a revolutionary, but not new, idea. Working for the good of others has been in place longer than space and time. It may be unique in the present workplace, but not out-of-the-blue to anyone with a working knowledge of the way of Jesus. Connected to such transforming power, servant leadership can transform the human workplace. But first it must transform us. And you'll see in the pages ahead that with regard to servant leadership, *the stuff of inner transformation is a big deal.*

My hope is that this book will be a companion on your journey of transformation into servant leadership. In the pages ahead you won't merely read about servant leadership; you will be guided into practices that will change your heart, strengthen your leadership, and transform your workplace.

I invite you to join me on the journey of inner renovation necessary for us to be the effective and ethical leaders we have dreamed of being.

What if pursuing this change and making small differences in your role as a leader is your calling? If millions of us take up this challenge and make small differences in our spheres of leadership, we could do enormous good for workers throughout the world.

Let's get started!

Next Steps for Servant Leaders

Think about it (reflection). What attracts you to the vision of servant leadership? Your own pain as the victim of leadership malpractice? Seeing others mistreated? Or do you have a more neutral motivation rooted in a vision of being a better leader? What difference might your motivations make? What are the potential strengths and weaknesses, opportunities and threats inherent in your motivations?

Try it (action/application). For the next couple of days, observe leaders and their actions. Ask yourself, *Why did they do this, say that, or fail to do another thing?* No judgment; just assessment—like a dentist might do at your semiannual checkup.

Evaluate the results (assessment). What did you discover about yourself in this process? Did any fears come to the surface? Did you find increased confidence in your assessments of leadership, of leadership theory? Maybe you even found increased motivation to grow as a servant leader. Simply observe and notice what is real without a lot of self-critique.

1

Reality, Revelation, and Power

> Kings like to throw their weight around and people in authority like to give themselves fancy titles. It's not going to be that way with you. Let the senior among you become like the junior; let the leader act the part of the servant.
>
> Luke 22:26 *The Message*

A colleague shouted at me across his living room: "You don't understand, Todd! That is not the real me!" I was his boss and was in his home in the suburbs of a large Southern city to investigate charges made against him by several people on his staff. They were accusing him of verbal abuse and generally oppressive forms of leadership. There were rumors that at home his wife was being treated even worse. For months leading up to this encounter I had tried to get to the bottom of the allegations. But this intelligent and slick man easily countered any report of wrong-doing with verbal clouds of fog so dense no one could see through them. Our tense dialogue in his home that day went on and on like that for a couple hours.

But then his wife spoke. *Finally!* I thought. With no prompting from me, she suddenly blurted out charges of physical abuse, consistent verbal attacks, and emotional turmoil at home. She went on to confirm what his employees were telling me. And, as almost always happens in these cases, she recounted to me her husband's frequent threats: "Don't tell anyone or you will ruin our ministry. Our kids will be devastated. Our extended families will no longer respect us. We will lose our ability to earn a living."

Those fearful sentences are not heavy clouds of fog designed to disorient accusers. They are molten rock spewed from the smoldering volcano of anger inside her husband. Why? He needed to control the people and events of his life at any cost. It was the only way he felt he could secure himself and insure the outcomes so dear to him. In a tragic irony, those hoped-for outcomes, even though they came wrapped in religious language, were the sparks that lit a great fire of the most irreligious behavior imaginable. Blindness to reality often exacts that toll.

For a wife wanting to make her marriage work, this man's hot words caused deep burns in her heart and soul. Upon hearing them I immediately reconsidered the irritated *Finally!* that had gone through my mind moments earlier. This guy was big. He stood over six feet, four inches tall and weighted at least 250 pounds. She was petite and carried herself softly. She had no chance against him. I realized I had just witnessed, in her confronting him, a profound act of courage.

He was busted. Nevertheless, he composed himself, scooted to the edge of his armchair, and with his eyes yearning and sincerity oozing from his face, pleaded: "But Todd: that is not the real me. You must believe me. That is not the *real* me!" He wanted me to believe that the *real* him was the one who wanted to be better, who made inner vows to "never do it again." To which I said, "No. The contrary is true. Your words and actions exuding from within you are the most reliable indicators of the unseen but powerful inner reality from which they come. They come from that interior world—unseen, but real—pushing, shoving, twisting, forcing, and cursing."

He never made his way to the kind of mental and spiritual health required for servant leaders. He could not find his way to dealing with the inner reality that drove him. I am sad to say that most of his fearful predictions of consequences came true. In that moment I saw in a profound way the need for servant leadership and the potential for human goodness inherent in it. His case is not all that unusual. Of course the facts and circumstances change in every incident of bad leadership. But I have been supervising leaders for more than thirty years and have never seen anyone grow into servant leadership who was not willing to look deeply and carefully—but with hope!—at the interior sources that energize and animate their actions, attitudes, and articulations.

Here is why this is true: servant leadership reveals the *unseen* spiritual reality on which the *seen* world of marketplaces, products, work, and workers depend. Jesus's teaching in Luke 22:26—"Let the senior among you become like the junior; let the leader act the part of the servant"—is not rooted in some kind of spiritual fad. He was training his first followers in a core value that would shape their work—humble servant leadership—no matter what title they might hold.

Why would Jesus say what he did in Luke 22:26? Doesn't he know that the *only* way to get things done in *the real world* is to throw your weight around? Is Jesus naive? Doesn't he know that servants get bullied while *real* leaders get rewarded?

This is most likely: Jesus knows something we don't. He comes from and thus teaches from a reality that we don't know. This invisible reality grounded Jesus as a servant leader. Through teachings like Luke 22:26 he introduced his team to this knowledge. Connecting to this reality and relying on it, according to Jesus, will inspire a leader to act the part of a servant.

This reality—Jesus's reality—is both spiritual and physical, and exists independent of our thinking or feelings about it. For example, what if you hopped in your car, late to a crucial appointment, and noticed your fuel is low? You decide to try to make it anyway. Truth is, your wish to make it to an appointment doesn't change the reality that there's only so much gas in the tank and that you'll likely not make it. Likewise, even though a child may think a cloud is made of cotton candy, it remains water vapor.

Reality is experienced as a routine and practical matter on a daily basis. It's that on which we can rely. When speaking about this from a stage, I often walk up and down the steps illustrating how I, through experience, rely on steps. I typically do this without conscious thought. The steps are there, they can bear my weight, and I know it. That is good enough knowledge on which to *act*. Knowledge requires trust. I step because I trust. I do it almost without thought.

However, we can have false and competing beliefs about reality. False beliefs can have devastating consequences, which are obvious. And we often have a hierarchy of beliefs that compete for our allegiance. For example, I may believe that smoking cigarettes causes lung cancer in many people. But I may also believe that I am the exception, and my smoking won't lead to lung cancer. Or I may believe that cancer strikes after smoking for decades, and I will quit smoking years before I am in danger. I also may believe that because I enjoy smoking cigarettes (for whatever reason), it's worth the risk of getting lung cancer thirty or forty years from now.

The teachings and way of following Jesus too often sit in our minds in a similar way. We suppose that what he teaches is true and good for us. But if we are honest, there are other things that compete with Jesus's teaching. It's not that we don't believe in Jesus, but in our hierarchy of beliefs we justify acting contrary to his teaching. Here's an analogy. When we are young our mother and school teachers tell us to eat plenty of vegetables like broccoli and cauliflower. And we know that they are telling us the truth. But the reality is we don't particularly like vegetables' tastes and textures, and don't intend to eat them, believing that we'll be all right anyway. As we grow older we rationalize this eating behavior through a variety of means. But when we become vitamin deficient (or develop lung cancer, in the case of smoking), we realize the folly of our errant ways, change our behavior, and encourage others not to live as we have!

Similarly, too many workplaces are sick because of errant leadership. Jesus's model of—and teachings about—servant leadership is the cure. The key is to match our beliefs to reality as presented by Jesus. This reality, our friend and ally, is a critical concept behind servant leadership.

Don't let your false beliefs cause you to lose confidence in or to skirt truth. Right belief (or *true* beliefs or *truth* or *knowledge*) has two components: (1) it corresponds to reality, and (2) produces confidence, which in turn yields a readiness to *act* on what we know is true and not merely *profess* it because we think we ought to.

The New Testament frequently calls for belief. *Belief* points to a reality much deeper than merely grasping something intellectually. Belief calls for *trust, confidence,* and *reliance* on what is learned. For instance, at the end of the Sermon on the Mount, arguably among Jesus's most famous teachings, he says,

> These words I speak to you are not incidental additions to your life, homeowner improvements to your standard of living. They are foundational words, words to build a life on. If you work these words into your life, you are like a smart carpenter who built his house on solid rock. Rain poured down, the river flooded, a tornado hit—but nothing moved that house. It was fixed to the rock.
>
> But if you just use my words in Bible studies and don't work them into your life, you are like a stupid carpenter who built his house on the sandy beach. When a storm rolled in and the waves came up, it collapsed like a house of cards. (Matthew 7:24-27 *The Message*)

In this book *reality* comes into play in two critical ways. First, we will work on the unseen parts of our heart, soul, mind, and will. Although these are invisible, they are real—they exist and can be known through their effects. They are the *reality* behind our text messages and emails, or our curses and blessings. I want you to be aware of the truth about your current inner world: good and bad, bent to servant leadership or twisted away from it.

Second, there is the material world of the workplace. It too is real. It is the fruit of the unseen reality that gives rise to it. For instance you read a nasty email on your computer screen (sight) or overhear a boss chewing out a colleague (sound). The world of the five senses is real.

Servant leaders must be able to face these and all realities; they cannot hide, bury their head, or pretend. We never need to be afraid of reality. The best servant leaders are those who learn to lead, in part, by becoming the kind of leader who models appropriate responses to reality.

Who Invented Servant Leadership?

You will never hear it said that servant leadership was invented in a prestigious MBA program, devised by a brilliant executive management team or formulated by a talented human resources division at a Fortune 100 company.

Robert Greenleaf was first to make the concept of servant leadership visible in the literature, and you could say he inserted servant leadership into conversations regarding theories of leadership and management. For this he, and those professors and writers he influenced, deserve our sincere respect and gratitude. That said, I suspect he would agree with me about the divine origin of servant hearts.[1]

At its core, servant leadership means to *lead for the sake of others*. I am a Christian, a follower of Jesus, and I believe that the world works as it does because it is designed by our Creator. A spiritual reality undergirds the material world. Being *others oriented* has been in play within the unseen reality of the trinitarian God since before time began. Thus, entering in to the practice of servant leadership expands our view of reality. And leaders have to decide whether they will align their hearts, minds, and souls with that reality.

What Does It Mean to Align Our Hearts as Servant Leaders?

Inspiring business speakers give us expert advice on how to create change in our various corporate cultures, which typically includes servant leadership. Then, the conference ends. We fight traffic on the freeway or long lines at the airport to get home. The next day we're road weary and sleep deprived. In our first hallway conversation back at work, we react with anger, indifference, or frustration. Why? Didn't we just learn the way of patience, love, and service to others?

No we didn't. Such things are matters of the heart. And matters of the heart are not talked about at most business conferences. The *heart* is too religious and too mysterious for the rational, logical, and pragmatic workplace. What boss would allow you three days off and pay for your travel, lodging, meals, and conference registration to *work on your heart*? Henry Cloud asks:

1. How much training have you had in developing the kind of character that will affect the results you get in the job?

2. How many retreats has your company taken you on to work on your "makeup" as a person?

3. How many courses in college or business school instructed you in the ways that you needed to grow as a person in order to make it in business?

4. What were you taught about character?[2]

Our Internet newsfeeds reveal the human cost of answering Henry's questions. The daily news features scandal, corruption, greed, and slander in the workplace. Our ability to work for the common good is at a historic low. Corruption is prevalent. These problems reflect distorted hearts.

Many people hate their jobs. Most people would be happy to have a job in which no one yelled, cursed at, or belittled them. You don't have to be hotshot business consultant to know that. Stand near any water cooler, hang around a coffee machine or linger in a hallway where "the real meetings take place" and you'll hear griping about management, laments about boring meetings, or general grumpiness. Tension-filled posturing fills the air. Why? Because people are inherently corrupt? No. The problem arises from the harm done by leaders who rely solely on *positional models* of leadership.

What do I mean by *positional models* of leadership? Some authors use the term *power models*. This is leadership that uses positional, authoritarian, or hierarchical power. Power leadership, usually motivated by some combination of fear, insecurity, anxiety, or ego, is self-serving and focused on self-gain. The power someone possesses, how to get more of that power and how to protect it are its chief concerns. The power model is used by those who want to climb the corporate the ladder.

Servant leadership, on the other hand, focuses on *persons*, not power. It concentrates on becoming the kind of person others intuitively trust. Servant leaders want what is good for others: employees, stockholders, customers, or vendors.

The practices associated with positional models of leadership produce and facilitate the grumpy, griping atmosphere described earlier. While not all stress is avoidable, workplace stress lowers workers' quality of life. Much unhappiness in the workplace comes not from the complexity and urgency of the task, but from the ways people are led—or rather misled—through leadership malpractice.

For instance, according to Gallup's 2013 "State of the American Workplace" report,

> Just 30 percent of employees are engaged and inspired at work. . . . A little more than half of workers (52 percent) have a perpetual case of the Mondays—they're present, but not particularly excited about their job.
>
> The remaining 18 percent are actively disengaged or, as Gallup CEO Jim Clifton put it in the report, "roam the halls spreading discontent." Worse, Gallup reports, those actively engaging employees cost the U.S. up to $550 billion annually in lost productivity.[3]

As the restless grumbling of employees becomes increasingly loud, bad attitudes are addressed with various perks in the workplace. Better coffee. Nicer break rooms. Onsite gyms. These and other conveniences have become the prescription for the dreadful disease of low morale. I'm not implying that these amenities or the motivation behind providing them are always wrong. Servant-led companies have provided these kinds of onsite benefits to good effect. But such efforts, commendable as they are, do not go far enough in fixing the pain now associated with the workplace. And sometimes the motivation behind these efforts is questionable. Some companies may be reacting to a bargaining process or a union demand. Servant-led companies (who likewise have to negotiate on issues and deal with unions) carefully observe what best serves their employees, and thus the company and its customers, and find practical and meaningful ways to respond.

Though many workers are thankful for these perks—whatever the motivation—the disease of workforce malaise is better fixed via the improved workplace environment created by servant leadership. Why? Because the perks response does not go nearly deep enough. As Kelli B. Grant stated on CNBC.com, "Free massages or beer on tap in the office kitchen doesn't make up for a boss who is a jerk."[4] Think about it. Many of us were raised by a screaming parent, taught by a grouchy teacher or coached by a loud-mouthed bully. Did the occasional treat undo how much we feared being near them?

Why are humiliation, threats, blaming, intimidation, and condescending remarks the default behaviors of so many leaders? Because many leaders need to win (and thus humiliate others), need to get their way (and thus threaten others), need to be seen in a positive light (and thus blame others), need to give good news to those they report to (and thus intimidate others into fudging reports when necessary), and need to be seen as powerful in every setting (and thus speak condescendingly to others).

Those who promote servant leadership have ethical concerns about and hopes for the workplace. We think kindness and caring behavior do not create soft leaders (soft in the sense of being unable to do the right thing or make hard decisions). Actually, kindness and care are fundamental to and underlie good decisions *and* healthy friendships, family, neighborhoods, and workplaces. In the long run, nothing good happens without kindheartedness. *Every act of leadership that can be done through anger, bullying, threatening, or misleading can be done better in servant-led ways.*

Servant leadership does not lack the ability to be candid, clear, or decisive when the occasion calls for it. In fact, servant leadership facilitates great decision making by getting leaders out of the false polarity of *autocratic* (power in the hands of one person) versus *democratic* (power shared among many) leadership. Mature servant leaders know how to be truly present to the people and the events of their lives. They know how to respond appropriately to a particular person and situation. Servant leaders are able to—out of love and care for others—gracefully move along the autocratic–participatory continuum.

Do You Hunger For a New Way of Leading?

You may be reading this book because you are enduring or perhaps recovering from personal pain suffered in the workplace. Maybe you want to find a way to become the kind of leader you wish others would be for you. Or you may admire the corporate cultures of well-known servant-led companies like Southwest Airlines, Popeyes Louisiana Kitchen, Chick-fil-A, Starbucks, Toro, Herman Miller, Datron World Communications and Whole Foods. What makes them different?

Do you hunger for a new way of leading? Do you admire servant leaders? Then it's time to begin the journey of heart transformation to servant leadership. It won't be long before those you work with will see a change as you lead from the inside out—*from the heart.*

Next Steps for Servant Leaders

Think about it (reflection). Begin the important work of searching your heart, of asking what you think is most real. What do you actually rely on as you go through your day? What, at present, is most real about the unseen parts of you? Currently, what in you best aligns with servant leadership? Where are you stuck in unhelpful attitudes, such as fear, anger, or anxiety?

Try it (action/application). For a day or two try this key practice: seek to be especially present to the people and events of your life. Focus on being with them. Listen. Notice. Observe. Be alert. Try a little empathy.

Evaluate the results (assessment). Did being truly present seem fearful to you or overwhelming? If so, what were you afraid of? Is it that you can't fix everything fast enough or good enough? Or that the complexities and pain of human life are beyond your capacity to respond? Maybe you noticed something positive, such as increased love and empathy for others. For now simply note your responses and how you may need to change and grow.

2

The Inward Journey

> Effective leadership starts on the
> inside. Before you can hope to
> lead anyone else, you have to
> know yourself.
>
> Ken Blanchard and Phil
> Hodges, *Lead Like Jesus*

In college I studied business. My degree is in human
resources management. Because my father was an accoun-
tant I tried that first, but I realized I was not good at
math and lacked the patience necessary to carefully balance
accounts. I snooped around finance and economics as well.
They were more interesting. But they also taxed my number-
challenged mind. Looking next to the marketing department,
I realized that I had a genuine fascination with what makes
human beings tick, what motivates people to purchase goods
and services. Later I found my real sweet spot in the social
psychology of the workplace, how leaders and followers work
together in good ways to produce good goods.

I first began to have insights into servant leadership while in college. I wanted to be a better captain of the baseball team but occasionally found myself unable to do or say the right thing. Further, I saw the horrible ways some coaches talked to athletes under the guise of motivation or correction. I witnessed athletes treating teammates or competitors in demeaning ways. I spent many quiet moments wondering, *Why do these things happen? Do they have to? Are they somehow intrinsic to success? Must I be a jerk to compete, to get things done? Do I have to decide between being ethical and effective? Can I be both?*

But my college baseball coach was different. Coach has stood tall in my mind for decades now because he had created an interior well of goodness from which his words and deeds naturally flowed. He could be tough, but I always knew he cared more about me than the game or any error I may have committed. He was present, not aloof like some professors and coaches I knew. Unlike the posturing often seen in high-level athletes and coaches, he was real; there was no pretense about him. This made him safe, trustworthy and someone I worked hard for.

From these experiences, good and bad, I developed a working hypothesis: *anyone who seeks to be a servant leader must begin an inward journey of the transformation of heart, will, mind, and soul. Interior renovation is the only process that produces genuine, consistent servant leaders.* But how do we become the kind of person who routinely acts in servant ways, from the heart?

This requires discerning our strengths and weaknesses accurately. And then, as self-motivated self-starters, we get to work watering and fertilizing our strengths, and ruthlessly dealing with our weaknesses. To become a servant leader requires cooperating with the grace and power of God in the transformation of all aspects of ourselves: heart, soul, mind, body, and will. This self-leadership will produce the authentic motivation and capacity to then serve others.

To do the requisite work toward inner transformation we must make Jesus our master in spiritual things. We must decide to place our trust and confidence in him, becoming his apprentice in living. Doing so will revolutionize our lives, our families, our relationships, and our places of work.

Let me say again for emphasis: relying on Jesus in this manner is the best path to authentic, coherent, and dependable servant leadership. This is a bold claim, but I know it to be true: Jesus is the best person in history from which to learn servant leadership. It's not even a close call. You may have heard the truism that leadership is simply *influence*. No one has ever had the influence that Jesus has had on humanity. Regarding Jesus's permanent world-shaping influence, Dallas Willard wrote,

> The route of education and law, which Plato (427-347 BC) and Aristotle (384-322 BC) tried to lay down, proved to be ineffectual for fallen human nature as it is. The Greeks needed to invite the Romans in to stop their fratricides. The route of careful soul-management, which Stoic and Epicurean philosophers later retreated into, more or less conceded the world to evil, and concentrated on telling individuals how to make life in a hellish world bearable. It was into this scene of intellectual despair that the community of Christ came, with its message of hope. . . . It was [a message] of the cross combined with *agape* love: love first from God, seen in the cross, and then love filling human beings in all the dimensions of their ordinary life.[1]

No leader has ever attempted or accomplished as much a

Jesus has. No product, no innovation—not cars, boats or airplanes, not the Internet or smartphones—comes close to the revolution in the human condition brought about by Jesus Christ.

No one in history nears his brilliance, authority, insight, power, and moral goodness. Why? He is *of* and *from* a different reality. He has always existed, before space and time, within the Trinity: God the Father, God the Son, and God the Holy Spirit.

Don't panic! This is not going to be a difficult-to-fathom theology book. We're just doing some groundwork. I want the genius of servant leadership to receive a fair hearing. Don't relegate it to the realm of management fads or the latest supervision techniques. Rather, I want to set forth servant leadership in a manner that propels you to make the kind of inner change necessary to be an effective servant leader. I want you to be a servant leader who actually delivers (as measured by the various metrics of your place of work), who exceeds what the boss is looking for during periodic evaluations, and whom others experience as for their good.

What's the Trinity Got to Do with Servant Leadership?

For our grounding in servant leadership, let's go back to the Trinity. In the words of one biblical author, humans "live and move and have our being" within a trinitarian universe (Acts 17:28), a world spoken into existence, sustained, and, in the future, perfected by God. The love—the positive will to do good for each member of the Trinity by the other members—defies easy description. No known love story will do; they all fall far short.

For instance, no member of the Trinity would ever think a bad thought about the other members. As coequals, each member admires, blesses, supports, empowers, inspires, and builds up the others. They have done this and will continue to do so for all eternity. These trinitarian attitudes, behaviors and practices may seem foreign. Though they seem to come from another reality, they are core to the rationale and practices of servant leadership. As a theological matter, the Trinity is hard to understand. However, the behaviors of the three persons of the Trinity are not hard to *understand*. They are hard to *live*. We need this trinitarian model because servant leadership is not primarily composed of cognitive concepts but *lived* practices in life's real settings and among real people.

How do the interrelations of the Holy Trinity create a rationale for servant leadership? If the loving interrelations of the Trinity are good enough, strong enough, and consistent enough to create and hold the world together, surely we can rely on this loving relationship as a model for relating to others in our various places of work. This concept is counterintuitive to many people. However, the incarnation of Jesus reveals to us the character and personal goodness of all the persons of the Holy Trinity. As Madeleine L'Engle writes, "to many people it is scandalous that the Lord of the universe should condescend to come to his people as an ordinary man, with every human restriction. Why would ultimate power choose to limit itself in such a humiliating fashion? Is this what love is really all about?"[2] In a word, yes. It is also the taproot from which the character and resulting fruit of servant leadership grow.

But that last sentence has to be understood as something more than mere religious rhetoric. Remember the stairs I spoke of in chapter one? No one thinks about them, much less worries about them. Rather, we simply place our weight on each step, trusting it without thought. Similarly, the eternal behaviors within the Trinity provide the ultimate moral foundation and model for would-be servant leaders. The Trinity demonstrates how to treat others whether they are shareholders, volunteers, peers, or employees.

Which do you suppose has the most lasting transformative power: a seminar on supervisorial trends in the marketplace, or alignment of one's heart, soul, mind and relational self with the Creator of the universe, living and leading as the triune Creator intended? I have made my choice for the latter and have seen it make all the difference in the world.

Servant Leadership Begins with Intention

Servant leadership doesn't sneak up on us. It's not like an impulse purchase while in line at the grocery store checkout. Our hearts and the way we talk aren't suddenly transformed. We don't lay down power or positional models of leadership without intention.

The passion and confidence to pursue servant leadership often comes from an assessment of leadership models we have experienced as painful or dysfunctional. We may see how these models hurt others or pollute the work atmosphere.

I experienced this shift in thinking in a meeting in the 1980s. I was often intellectually, emotionally, and relationally shutting down while in meetings or during important conversations. I recognized that my problem was self-criticism. I didn't have the courage to say out loud what I was really thinking. I did not have the strength of character to be a servant leader in the presence of other leaders.

At the same time I started to realize this about myself as a senior leader: intense changes were happening in my corporate culture. New leaders were making revisions to our core values and practices. I believed these deviations were wrong for us and for the people we served.

But in high-level meetings I would look at the people sitting at the table, and these thoughts would run through my head: *He is smarter by accident than I am on purpose. She is one of the most spiritual people I know; she probably has some insight I lack. He is a famous author and speaker; who am I? He is my boss and mentor, and has done nothing but good for me, how can I contradict him? It would embarrass him in front of these other big shots!* Round and round my mind would go, finding ways to diminish my own intellect, my gifts, my love for the organization, its mission, and its future.

Articulating one's truest thoughts is a big deal, because no one can be a leader, much less a servant leader, without the ability to articulate a clear vision in a setting where others don't see what that person sees. A servant leader must stand up for a value system that undergirds the vision, and insist on the practices that bring the vision to reality. Becoming an excellent servant leader on the outside begins as a difficult inward journey.

Leadership from Inside Out

A leader is known by the effect he or she has on others. An apple tree is known by its fruit. It does not produce bananas. Likewise, a leader with the DNA of power, control, and lack of concern for others cannot produce an environment of service and care. There is a consistency between what is most real inside us—our inner DNA—and the behaviors and words that leak out under enough pressure.

This is why external approaches to changing one's leadership style will not work. We can't unclog the arteries of our hearts by taking a shower. A shower, no matter how delightful and cleansing, leaves the inside untouched. We may *look* fresh, but nothing has changed *inside* us. The real problem is the clogged and dirty places of our hearts. To cleanse and heal our hearts takes a different strategy.

Many people, not just leaders, try to cover their spiritual, emotional, and psychological deadness by cleaning their exterior. This isn't effective. Not for long, anyway! Eventually, the inner reality will be manifest: a heart dead to loving and serving others.

This reveals the most difficult truth on the inner journey toward servant leadership: our *outward* actions and words are reliable indicators of what exists within. This truth has guided the wise for two thousand years.[3]

Working on outward behavior alone, which is popular in leadership training, is dysfunctional. It leaves would-be leaders feeling confused and hypocritical. They don't want to act in ways they now know are wrong. They want to be mature servant leaders. But they realize that merely hearing servant leadership ideas does not enable the fundamental inner change needed to alter behavior.

This realization can lead to feelings of impotence and hopelessness regarding internal change. Human change happens from the inside out. The inner world of the human heart controls the outer world of actions and speech. Yet corporations, schools, and the government try to change human behavior on the outside while ignoring the heart. Without addressing the heart we either don't change at all or we change temporarily, act inconsistently, get frustrated with the process, and quit.

Worst of all, if we succeed on the outside without the corresponding inward change, we inadvertently become worse kinds of human beings: self-righteous and judgmental. But eventually we grow deeply frustrated because we soon recognize we are play acting. The people we lead see through the façade and accuse us of being hypocrites. We are now worse off than when we began.

In today's workplace, leaders and workers are angry, increasingly uptight, and judgmental. Trying to find some way to survive, workers become manipulators and less loving. It doesn't take a psychologist or a religious leader to know that those traits are not the appropriate building blocks of character.

"Well then," you ask, "how do I learn servant leadership? How do I get it right?" Servant leadership is *self-authenticating*. You will know it, you will confirm its substantive goodness, as you begin to practice it. You've probably been the recipient of it from a good leader. On the giving side, maybe you've had moments—beautiful, freeing moments—when you behaved and spoke from your highest and best self.

Though the notion that human change happens from the inside out comes from Jesus, this does not make it a mere religious idea. Jesus, the most sophisticated and moral leader of all time, towers above all cultures and cannot be rendered obsolete by today's widespread cynicism about religion. On the contrary, Jesus's teachings are solidly connected to the real world. His teaching on servant leadership is true of all humans in all places and at all times. The perceptiveness and comprehension shown by Jesus are why it was said of him: "The people were amazed at his teaching, because he taught them as one who had authority, not as [their usual teachers]" (Mark 1:22). *Authority* in this context means, "That guy has real expertise" or "He says weighty things" or "His words have power and surreal influence."

Jesus's words come from another, truer and more concrete reality. They are meant to reshape human reality, beginning with the transformation of our hearts.

Are you beginning to see now how this works? When I had an epiphany about the inner realities that controlled my leadership practices, it shattered my courage, confidence, and poise. From this experience, I was led to a lifelong journey of inner change for the sake of those I serve and lead.

Here is the bottom line of leadership development: Our hearts are a mix of good and bad habits, of great potential, and seemingly unalterable weaknesses. Our inner persons are hard drives of memories and motivations married to hopes and dreams, as well as doubts and fears. You cannot be a servant leader without taking a deep look at—and healing—your heart.

Jesus, the all-time most brilliant person on this subject, makes the theme of this chapter perfectly plain: "A good man brings good things out of the good stored up in him, and an evil man brings evil things out of the evil stored up in him" (Matthew 12:35).

With this knowledge in hand, formerly mysterious things become open and clear. Genocides. School shootings. Bombings. Gang rapes. Brutal killings. Rampant spying and lying within and between national governments. Teachers who have sex with their underage students. These are not flukes. They perfectly exhibit the hearts of the perpetrators.

But the human heart does not merely motivate in ruthless, negative ways. Think of the heroes who save their neighbors from drowning during storms. We can see their hearts through their actions. Think of the actions of the police, firefighters, medical responders, ordinary people who pull strangers from burning cars, those who give to the homeless, those who care for the poor or who show special respect to the elderly. Attitudes and actions like these are the outflow of what is in the heart.

Growth, Not Perfection

At this point you may be thinking, "Ya, ya, ya . . . blah, blah, blah. I got it! But does servant leadership make business sense? My boss and my board of directors, or my donors, or my shareholders expect real results."

I understand that line of questioning. I live in the same world. And I am convinced servant leadership is the best form of leadership for all stakeholders and for the basic metrics of your business or enterprise. You may find yourself beginning to agree with me. But I also know how it feels to first consider these big ideas. I remember the self-doubt. I recall wondering if others would think I was crazy. I wondered if I could really pull it off.

A word of encouragement: Don't worry too much about the habitual faults you identify in yourself or in your leadership. All of us on the journey to servant leadership start with handicaps of some sort. Where we start from is important. We should realistically and humbly recognize our weaknesses and remain alert to them as we grow as servant leaders. But where we begin is not the decisive factor in how well we pick up the attitudes, beliefs, and practices associated with servant leadership.

The decisive factors are:

» gaining a compelling vision for servant leadership for yourself and your leadership team

» deciding with firm intention to go for it

» finding the practical resources, ways, and means for carrying out—little by little—your intention

Don't become overly concerned about the need to have a perfect heart. In the work we are doing together in this book, *perfection* is never on the table. *Growth* is. None of us can be perfect, and servant leadership does not require it. But it does require a growing connection to reality—inwardly to your heart and outwardly to the people and events of your life—within the present rhythms and routines of your work.

So don't use "I can't be perfect" as an excuse for a failure to grow. All of us can grow, and when we do, the workplace becomes a slightly better place. But *slightly* multiplied by thousands of leaders makes a discernible impact on others, on those who are our followers. Consistent leadership behaviors, not mere words in meetings or plaques on walls, assure followers: "You *do* care about me! I *can* trust you! You *will* help me and not merely use me!"

Power

Servant leadership is a philosophy and a particular approach to leadership. It also involves a specific set of leadership practices. But who would value and hold such a philosophy? Who really practices servant leadership consistently? Only the person with a particular set of beliefs and attitudes in his or her heart.

For instance, when someone believes leaders must amass power, that leads to zero-sum thinking and power grabbing as the platform for leadership. Those beliefs don't stay hidden. They appear in meetings, phone calls, and emails. Positional models pollute a corporate culture from the get-go. Servant leadership is not so much the *exercise* of power as it is the *creation* of a steady stream of power. It does not employ zero-sum thinking, which creates winners and losers. Servant leadership knows power can be shared, thus empowering everyone's work life.

But servant leadership is not *hands-off* or *laissez-faire*— the deliberate abdication or withdrawal of leadership so that *things take their own course* without direction or interference from a leader. While *laissez-faire* leadership can be good, right, and valuable in specific settings (i.e., a focused, motivated, trustworthy, and experienced team of experts), servant leadership is normally far from merely *letting things go*.

In the phrase *servant leadership*, the word *servant* is a modifier of *leadership*. Leadership is assumed. Far from *letting things go*, influencing the future in positive ways is the function of leader. But a servant leader leads from a set of assumptions significantly different from the power or positional norms known in most workplaces. Of most importance he or she is a servant first. Serving others—employees, vendors, bankers, investors, shareholders, clients, and customers—is the servant leader's primary instinct.

An All-Powerful Model

Humility, defined as accurate self-knowledge, is at the core of a servant leader's confidence. Once again, we can do no better than the model of Jesus:

> Jesus knew that the Father had put him in complete charge of everything, that he came from God and was on his way back to God. *So* he got up from the supper table, set aside his robe, and put on an apron. Then he poured water into a basin and began to wash the feet of the disciples, drying them with his apron . . .
> Then he said, . . . so if I, the Master and Teacher, washed your feet, you must now wash each other's feet. I've laid down a pattern for you. What I've done, you do. (John 13:3-5, 12-14 *The Message*)

What a powerful model! "Yes," you might say, "but how do I do that?" I'll say more in the chapters ahead, but for now did you notice the two-letter word *so*, which I italicized? It is the logical and heart-based rationale and drive behind Jesus's easy and relaxed service of others. He knew who he was, where he had come from and where he was going. Armed with that interior knowledge, as he washed his coworkers feet he gave perhaps the greatest illustration of servant leadership.

What do you suppose would be the condition of the heart and soul of the leader who sought to serve others? We see what oriented Jesus: He came from God—the Trinity—secure in the wholly trustworthy and competent love of God. This secure love gave him the confidence to risk being misunderstood in order to serve others.

The servant leader's heart needs to be similarly animated and energized. In chapter three we will keep at it little by little, because, as T. S. Eliot wrote in *The Four Quartets*, "Humankind cannot bear very much reality."[4]

Next Steps for Servant Leaders

Think about it (reflection). Begin to think about God—a Trinity of persons who are by nature completely competent love. What can you imagine about the relational love that exists among the three persons of the Trinity? How do you suppose perfectly powerful and loving persons would treat each other? Can you imagine such love animating the attitudes, deeds, and words of human leaders? What might it look like in practice or sound like in conversation?

Try it (action/application). For the next week, find at least one setting or conversation in which you ask yourself, *What would be the loving thing to do?* Then do it. Make sure you are not doing it to be seen by others. Make sure the loving act or word is genuine and done for the good of another.

Evaluate the results (assessment). What affect did your loving actions have on you? How did you feel about yourself? What did you notice about the reaction of the recipients? Were they grateful? Did they cynically assign wrong motives you? What did you learn about servant leadership through this exercise?

3

The Heart of the Matter

Our companies can never be
anything we do not want ourselves to be.

Max De Pree,
Leadership Is an Art

"Houston, we have a problem . . ." Maybe that
famous line helps you call to mind the movie
Apollo 13. Do you remember the mission
control room, its rows of gray metal desks rising from the
floor in an amphitheater-like room? They surround the large
screen at the front of the room. The men and women at those
desks, working *out of sight*, controlled the crew and what was
happening to the spacecraft *in space*.

Our hearts are like that. They are like the chief executive
officer of our being. From our *out-of-sight* hearts there flows
naturally an *in space* or *in public* kind of person and thus a

kind of leader. This is a law of leadership as strong as the law of gravity. Let me show you what I mean.

A person who once worked for me was raised in a deeply troubled home. Like many children in that situation he learned very effective survival skills. He learned how to manipulate, bully, threaten, and embarrass others in order to get his way. Whenever he cared a great deal about something or someone, he pulled out those big guns from their inner holsters and brandished them in the air. Why? Because underneath an intelligent and competent exterior there was a little boy needing to know that someone loved him, that he would not be abandoned by everyone, that he was someone to be valued, respected, and admired.

Those thoughts were the software running his automatic responses to life and leadership. And because the heart is the locker room of the game, the rehearsal hall of the play, the situation room of the White House, he was often dismissive of others and used the power of his intellect to control or belittle colleagues.

The mouth speaks what the heart ponders. What is being pondered in the heart of a leader guilty of poor leadership? Thoughts like this: *I might get hurt here. I must secure myself by controlling the environment, by using my power to govern the responses of others. If I don't protect myself, my vision, and my goals, no one will.*

What about the interior life of the servant leader pursuing spiritual transformation into Christlikeness? While no one is perfect, it's normally something like this: *I am always safe in the kingdom of God. The Lord is my Shepherd; I therefore do not have to hurt others in order to make myself safe. Be still and know that God is Lord of this situation.*

This may seem a bit idealistic. Can anyone really get to this point? Yes! We get there through the combination of the grace and power of God, and our behind-the-scenes training to love and serve with excellence. We are slowly transformed so that on the spot—in the meeting, on the difficult call, or when unfairly treated at work—we can speak and behave as servant leaders.

To get there, we must first embrace this idea: servant leadership demands a journey of spiritual transformation. I have been on that journey for a long time. It is sometimes painful to acknowledge, precisely name, and confront the parts of my heart and soul that are twisted into anxious, angry, selfish knots. But looking back over my journey, lots of creative good was born from understanding my darkness and pain.

My experience is not shared by everyone. Sometimes the pains of leadership lead to addiction to painkillers such as alcohol, drugs, lavish consumption, sexual immorality.

A big part of our personal growth as servant leaders depends on unlearning the false thinking we bring into our daily lives. For this we need a teacher. Who should teach us about the heart, soul, mind, and will of servant leadership? While respectfully acknowledging the truth found in many philosophies and religious traditions, I believe Jesus has the most extensive and valuable perspective, the truest insights and best information possible on servant leadership. He is the world's foremost example.

The chief criticism of servant leadership is that it is grounded on the person and teaching of Jesus, so it is not applicable to leaders in today's secular workplaces. Jesus is set aside because he is *God*, and thus not a human model, or he's *ancient*, and thus ignorant of the modern, complex global scene. He's too mystical, spiritual, or religious, and not practical enough.

But what if the opposite is true? What if he is the most brilliant person to have ever lived? What if Jesus knows how to lead human beings in *every* human endeavor? Do you think he is at least as smart as you? Would Jesus waffle if he walked into a room of PhDs in leadership from MIT, Harvard, Stanford, Wharton, or Yale? Would he be intimidated by them? What if Jesus is the most natural, intuitive, and capable leader ever?

Reflect on these passages by Dallas Willard, who was a professor of philosophy at the University of Southern California:

> You can be very sure that nothing fundamental has changed in our knowledge of ultimate reality and the human self since the time of Jesus. . . . The multitudes of theories, facts, and techniques that have emerged in recent centuries have not the least logical bearing upon the ultimate issues of existence and life. . . .
>
> It is not possible to trust Jesus in matters where we do not believe him to be competent.
>
> And can we seriously imagine that Jesus could be Lord if he were not smart? If he were divine, would he be dumb? Or uninformed?
>
> In the ethical domain He had an understanding of life that has influenced world thought more than any other.
>
> "Jesus is Lord" can mean little in practice for anyone who has to hesitate before saying "Jesus is smart." He is not just nice. He is brilliant. He is the smartest man who ever lived. He is now supervising the entire course of world history while simultaneously preparing the rest of the universe for our future role in it. He always has the best information on everything and certainly on the things that matter most in human life.[1]

Does this portrayal of Jesus shock you? Maybe you can't wrap your head around it. Perhaps you have trouble believing it is true. These initial reactions are reasonable. Sometimes shocking information is life altering. You've heard of guys who, having received a diagnosis of lung cancer, never pick up another cigarette. Or the woman who crashes her car, narrowly avoiding the DUI she knows she deserved, and never drinks again. Those are the moments we become open to change, open to working on the heart of a matter.

Training for Servant Leadership

The concept of an inward journey that leads to the heart of servant leadership is not something I made up. I learned it from my Teacher. He is a Master in what it means to be a servant. These brilliant insights illustrate Jesus's grasp on the source, cause, and basis of human behavior:

> A good tree cannot bear bad fruit, and a bad tree cannot bear good fruit. (Matthew 7:18)

> Make a tree good and its fruit will be good, or make a tree bad and its fruit will be bad, for a tree is recognized by its fruit. (Matthew 12:33)

> You clean the outside of the cup and dish, but inside they are full of greed and self-indulgence. . . . First clean the inside of the cup and dish, and then the outside also will be clean. (Matthew 23:25-26)

> You are like whitewashed tombs, which look beautiful on the outside but on the inside are full of the bones of the dead and everything unclean. (Matthew 23:27)

In the rough-and-tumble environments found in commerce, politics, education and other places of human work, the heart, which to Jesus was the interpretive key to all human behavior, is neglected. Compared to professional knowledge and skills, it gets little attention. Yet to ignore the heart—the human interior—is to ignore a critical component of our lives. Like the invisible software system running my word processing program, our hearts are the behind-the-scenes operating systems that drive our attitudes, actions, and words. Our hearts rule us. A person doesn't have to be a religious fanatic to see the pattern Jesus describes. Our *outward* words and actions are reliable indicators of what exists within our *inner* selves.

Jesus taught the public leaders of his day that their fundamental approach to spirituality and leadership was flawed and dysfunctional. *Trying to change human behavior while ignoring the heart never works.* Yet this method persists in corporations, classrooms, hospitals, and small businesses.

Let's look at New Year's resolutions as an example. You've made them. So have I. And what have we observed? That New Year's resolutions are rarely kept. Right? Why? Because *direct effort of the will* to control how much food goes on our forks, or how much we gossip, or how much wine we drink, does not work. Willpower, while a good and God-given thing, can't create lasting change by itself. Our thoughts and emotions badger and nag our will to give us what we want, thereby trumping our resolutions. Our thoughts pester us with how good things would be if we would just give in to desire.

We need indirect effort. We need to *train* ourselves, not just *try harder*, to control a broken interior life. Our *wanters*, the interior source of our desires, need to be trained *off the spot* in order to be able to do the right thing *on the spot.*[2] The *inward transformation of the heart* changes our relationship to food, the need to gossip, or the need to medicate pain with various vices.

Heart Issues

What does Jesus mean when he speaks of the "heart"? Our inner controlling mechanism. For instance, Jesus taught that "the mouth speaks what the heart is full of" (Matthew 12:34). Summarizing his argument, Jesus contends that "A good man brings good things out of the good stored up in him, and an evil man brings evil things out of the evil stored up in him" (Matthew 12:35).

A wonderful example of how our heart and our desires control us when we're under pressure is illustrated in the New Testament Gospels. In Matthew 26 we read that during the last part of Jesus's life he made a lot of political and religious enemies. The crowds who followed Jesus were nervous, and his best friends began to wonder where it was all going.

Jesus told his friends that he would be betrayed by one of them. Peter confidently retorted that even if all Jesus's friends fell apart under the pressure, he would remain steadfast. Yet, just as Jesus predicted, Peter disowned Jesus. Peter's inner desire for safety and security quickly and easily overpowered his outward vow.

I believe Peter was telling Jesus the truth. I don't think he was bragging or being carelessly boastful. I think he meant what he said. He simply did not have the inner resources to keep his promise. This is a crucial insight for those who want to be servant leaders. Many would-be servant leaders make inner vows to be kind, honest, or humble only to respond as Peter did.

I'll stop picking on Peter, and pick on me for a moment. I *say* I highly value peace and a slow, quiet pace of life. I often tell colleagues and friends, "Hurry is not *of* the devil, it *is* the devil!" Or "I need to ruthlessly eliminate hurry from my life!"[3]

But my calendar reveals that I'm not doing what I say I value! I *think* I mean what I say. I'm not intentionally lying. But the disconnect between my stated intention and the state of my heart leads me to reflect on my *true* posture. I ask myself,

» Why can't I say no?

» Why do I want to be needed more than I want my stated values and notional convictions?

» Why is it important that people notice, value, and comment on my contributions?

» Why do I have such a high need for constant achievement?

» Why does doing nothing drive me crazy and make me feel unproductive?

Sadly, I could go on. These are the heart issues I constantly work on. I have had some success in addressing these through an inner dialogue that includes questions such as, What if my work is not the most important thing? What if I cannot be reduced to my work? Maybe from God's view my work is not his work? Maybe I, the kind of person I become in carrying out my leadership, am his work?

Coming to understand that your *first* realm of work is to

cooperate with God in the transformation of your soul is one of the greatest insights you can gain. I am God's main work. My daily work is the soil in which I am meant to grow as a follower of Jesus, as a husband, as a father and as a servant leader. This kind of daily self-talk reliably takes me back to heart work: mind, soul, will, imagination, and the vision and priorities I have for my life. And when I live as if *I* am God's work, I find deep love and patience. I discover clarity and focus. I have energy and an artfulness that is not available to me in any other way.

The Anxious Heart

Ken Blanchard and Phil Hodges are important voices in the servant leadership conversation. Ken has spent four decades consulting in most every aspect of the human workplace. His coauthor, Phil, is an expert in human resource management. They write that most approaches to leadership development "try to improve one's leadership style and methods. Emphasis is on the *hands* of the leader. They attempt to change leadership from the outside. Yet . . . we have found that effective leadership starts on the inside; it is a *heart* issue."[4] Blanchard and Hodges go on to assert that the most persistent barrier to becoming a servant leader is "a heart motivated by self-interest," which is antithetical to a heart bent toward the good of others.

Here's another way to think about it. You've probably heard, or remarked yourself, "I wish so-and-so would live up to his beliefs!" What if all of us live up to our *actual* beliefs? Go back for a moment to my battle with nonstop work. I *say* I believe in quiet rest, but I apparently believe that I need constant achievement. Maybe what we don't live up to, and others notice, is our *stated* beliefs. Often our *stated* beliefs are not our *actual* and *deep* beliefs. Servant leaders have to do the work of drilling down to their real beliefs. These subterranean beliefs have a firm grasp on the steering wheel of our attitudes, actions, and words.

Let me explain what I mean. Aiming to say what he or she believes, a person can state sincerely, "I trust God!" But as soon as this person feels unsafe, he or she resorts to old patterns. These behaviors that reveal the true heart can manifest themselves as manipulation, bullying, or obscuring the truth. They may also cause us to hide out of fear, or abuse various substances to dull the anxiety that comes from refusing to trust God.

Isolating ourselves from people who might hurt us or prove untrustworthy can give us a sense of power, of control over our lives. But such behavior simultaneously shrinks our lives. Besides: *we cannot be servant leaders if we are afraid of people.* However, our fear of people can be conquered if we are willing to go on the inner journey of learning to love people from a secure and more confident heart.

Substance abuse works in much the same way: it dulls the pain of anxiety but shrinks our lives as we increasingly hide our behavior from others, including spouses and members of our family. Again, with help, servant leaders develop a heart that can deal with pain and become an agent of healing. They do not run from pain by altering their brain chemistry. Rather, like firefighters racing to a conflagration, they run into places of pain, serving from a heart of humble, gentle confidence.

What are we to make of this outward–inward duality? Are the vast majority of us baldfaced liars? Hypocrites? No. We are out of touch with our heart, our true center. This is what makes our behaviors inconsistent with our stated beliefs. We get out of touch with ourselves because we live on the surface of life. We rush with manic speed from meeting to meeting, or from long commutes to kids' activities, and rarely connect with our true but below-the-surface values, which powerfully control our behaviors.

We say we are confident, but our broken, frightened hearts win the day over theoretical values. From this inconsistency come defensive remarks and putdowns. We are not hypocrites. We are not phonies, pretenders, or posers. We simply do not understand the inner drivers of our lives. Servant leaders can't live this way. We have to get to the heart of the matter.

Tackling the Issues

There are innumerable variations of inner conflicts that need to be addressed on the journey of servant leadership:

» Servant leaders need to be consistent, but I am moody and fickle.

» Servant leaders need to be confident, but I am fearful and unsure.

» Servant leaders need to be fair, but I am angry and erratic.

» Servant leaders need to be honest, but I am manipulative and fudge the truth.

Let me show you how to work on a single issue. Suppose you want to be more plainspoken and honest in conversations, without verbal acrobatics designed to make sure you win the argument or get your way. Take an inner inventory. Perhaps you notice that you fear work-related consequences or relational distress over what others may think of you. This is the hidden heart reality that drives you to *power speaking* rather than *servant speaking*.

That is a potent and compelling bit of self-awareness—but what do you do next? Try this: at least once a day for a week or a month, practice intentionally letting go of control by setting aside controlling or bullying statements. Deliberately make yourself vulnerable. Take a back seat and let others have the last word. You can do this in ways that don't endanger your work or those you work with. Try not to bring undue attention to yourself when you do this. And then, without judging yourself, simply notice what happens in your inner person and how you feel about it. You won't die. The earth will continue to spin. And your work will go on.

You will quickly learn that in normal noncrisis circumstances, servant words are actually more effective than power words. You will discover that "right action is freedom," as T. S. Eliot wrote, and "in my end is my beginning."[5] When you fully trust Jesus, confidently following his teaching, you are safe even when you use simple language that allows others to hold on to their opinions and leaves them in charge of their minds and their lives.

That is behavior of the highest character. That is servant leadership.

Next Steps for Servant Leaders

Think about it (reflection). Take a moment to think about your current leadership practices. Choose your most consistent failing and those incidences when you don't live up to your stated ideals, morals, or standards of behavior. Now identify your favorite compliment people give you regarding your leadership. Becoming aware of whatever you can in this moment, write down the heart issues that motivate both sets of practices. Sit quietly for a few moments and recollect concrete situations when you acted negatively in contrast to your stated beliefs. Notice what you were feeling. Try to assess your real heart in the way I modeled regarding my busyness. Struggle against the default position that "for most of us there is only the unattended moment," and attend to what was going on internally, probably subconsciously.[6]

Try it (action/application). Pick one inconsistent weakness to work on over the next week or month. For example, I find one or two times a day to become completely still and silent. It may be for only a few minutes, but it recalibrates my thinking, attitudes, and actions. You can't work on several servant leadership issues at the same time. The pace of inner transformation is slow. It requires keen focus. Anxiously thinking about several heart issues at one time will blunt real transformation. Don't try to tackle to broad range of challenges. Pick one and go deep for a long period of time. You will be surprised by the transformative power of such focus.

Evaluate the results (assessment). When you apply indirect effort (such as being still in order to reorient your heart against hurry) against your weakness, or leverage it against your best strength, what do you notice happening within you? Do you notice any new or different reactions from your workmates? What do these observations teach you? For instance, sometimes battling my propensity to hurry, I notice that I am not really present to the people and events of my life. Or I become aware of a subconscious fear or lack of confidence.

Once stillness brings those feelings to my conscious mind, I can be honest about them before God and deal with them in peace. What do you notice about yourself as you practice what I suggest?

4

Training the Character

> Put everything you have into the
> care of your heart—the hidden,
> causative, motivational you—
> for everything you do flows from
> it. . . . It is the real source of your
> outward life. . . . It determines
> what your life amounts to.
>
> Proverbs 4:23,
> author's paraphrase

I slammed my hand on the steering wheel so hard it hurt my wrist. Why? Toward the end of writing this book I was going through a challenging time. Nothing in my various places of work was going well. Everything was harder, slower, and more complex than I thought it needed to be. At the end of a long week and a long Saturday of work I needed to exercise, engage in some self-care, blow off some steam, and get my mind on something positive.

On my way to my favorite hobby, worried, frustrated,

and distracted by the huge challenges in my leadership roles, I accidentally passed my off-ramp on the freeway. My hand struck the steering wheel as I looked at the clock and saw that my mistake was going to make me late. A few seconds later I looked up to see a normal Southern California sight: red brake lights for miles. Then in double anger I slammed the roof of the car with my fist.

This was rare, even scary, behavior for me. Normally I am very even-tempered. So the unusual outburst got my attention: *What the heck! What is wrong with you?* At that moment I remembered the most profound definition of anger: Anger is "a response towards those who have interfered with us. It includes a will to harm them, or the beginnings thereof."[1] At that moment I felt great empathy for leaders who live daily with that kind of anger. I felt sad for them and for those "their will to harm" has indeed harmed. I realized that even though as a follower of Jesus I have worked on my inner self a great deal, I was still capable of acting out with violence. Thank God the steering wheel and roof of the car are plastic and metal! Sometimes leadership malpractice animated by anger hurts a person with a tender heart, a timid mind, or a loving soul.

How do servant leaders respond to the normal anger-producing moments of life? They first think of the Other and others. In a split second—this is a wonder of our mental capacity!—before they open their mouths, knowing that "The tongue has the power of life and death" (Proverbs 18:21), they ponder, *How would I want to be treated or spoken to in this situation?* Or *What would I not want done to me in this circumstance?*

What kind of person can routinely act with such thoughtfulness? I understand the question and the perplexed place it comes from. For this is the reality: the challenges presented by developing the character of a servant leader are not like the intellectual demands of rocket science, software development, international relations, or brain surgery. They are far more challenging (but in a different way)! Our hearts and characters have a trajectory or bent, which grows in a definite direction. Think of it as a rose plant climbing over an arch. From childhood we are often malformed by hurt, indifference, or abuse. Adolescence usually brings disappointments or even derailments from a hoped-for goal. In adulthood, our hearts and our characters may be formed by cynicism and regrets—all leading to the kind of anger and other dysfunctional patterns of leadership discussed earlier. (In our quest for servant leadership, not all life experiences are malforming. But here we are working to train the wrongly bent parts of our hearts in a new direction.)

Let's be clear: there are no perfectly suited servant leaders. All of us have attributes that tilt in the right direction and kinks that twist us in the wrong way. This simply means we are living, breathing people with issues we need to work on. The key is to understand and be present to what is real in you and in others. This will help you catch yourself before you do or say something hurtful or stupid, which in turn pollutes your corporate culture or causes you to lose a productive, cherished employee.

Servant leadership requires a commitment to serious personal growth and development. Before we can become transformational leaders, we must first be transformed ourselves. Those who have tried to change a core part of who they are know that direct effort does not work—at least not deeply or for long. Directly trying to wrestle and overpower our inner selves always lead to frustration. Simply trying harder—struggling against the way we are bent—will only exhaust us. Long term, it will never work.

Trying to *act* as a servant leader without *heart* change—the inner disposition to do so—is bound to come off as the newest management fad—fake or hypocritical. The best leaders take the time (slow down!) to develop the persistence, patience, discipline, and inner transformation that will result in being servant leaders. We must become *the kind of people* who naturally and routinely—as a matter of habit—function as servant leaders, who love and generously give to others the workplace gifts of trust, respect, listening, and relationship.

We all know the frustration of trying to get better at something. For instance, we decide to run to lose weight. We go out with enthusiasm, only to come limping back with sore muscles, a pounding heart, and heaving lungs. Our bodies scream: *Stop! This is not for you! This is for skinny people! You're going to hurt yourself or have a heart attack!* Ironic, isn't it? Some messages we hear clearly and quickly obey!

Whether you are running a marathon or becoming a servant leader, you prepare and train yourself into a new reality—a different way of being—by the steady transformation of your current self. Servant leadership requires a new *kind* of learning. It is heart-level stuff, by far the hardest kind of change. A mental grasp of the *ideas* of servant leadership is only the beginning. Initial servant leadership concepts, theories, ideals, and models function to give us the first needed ingredient: a vision, a glimpse of a preferred future.

After receiving the vision and making at least a hypothetical commitment to it, we must assess our current state.

Appendix two has a more thorough model, but for now you can assess yourself over several weeks by taking a few moments each evening to review your day. Try this:

1. Look back and observe today's actions. Pay attention to your body language. Did you project anger, peace, humble confidence, or _____?

2. Evaluate your conversations. Were your words meant for the good of others? Or were they motivated by fear, insecurity, and a need to be right or completely in control?

Personal growth of all kinds—in music, learning a new language, or in sports—always begins with this sort of assessment. This is why coaches are so important. The best coaches are expert observers. They detect things we don't see about ourselves. If you can afford a servant leadership coach, get one. (The Servant Leadership Institute can help you with this—see information at the back of this book.) If you can't afford one, commit to coach someone at work and have him or her coach you in return. It will help you more than you might think!

For example, you may recognize that you have a short fuse in stressful situations. Have you ever wondered why some people get to the place where they rely on anger to function as leaders? Here are a couple of reasons to consider: the adrenaline associated with anger makes me feel strong. It gives me the inner fuel to act or speak. Yes—okay. All of us have felt a similar mal-motivation at times. But what should you do if you have fallen into this as a pattern of behavior? I can tell you this: *You won't change by trying harder.* You have to be trained in anger management. Anything you can accomplish via anger can be accomplished better without it. One of the leaders Jesus trained in servant leadership wrote this:

> My dear brothers and sisters, take note of this: Everyone should be quick to listen, slow to speak and slow to become angry, because human anger does not produce the righteousness that God desires. Therefore, get rid of all moral filth and the evil that is so prevalent and humbly accept the word planted in you, which can save you. (James 1:19-21)

This passage contains a huge and consequential idea: Human anger cannot produce human flourishing in the home, in friendships, or in the workplace. But when you learn to lead with your ears—ears attached to a heart that is committed to the good of others—leading from anger naturally falls away like old skin cells making way for new life.

What if leading from anger, from the need to be in control or from greed is *moral filth*? What if it is destroying the souls of leaders and their followers? If you are tracking with me in believing that such leadership is a big problem, then let's keep working together to "humbly accept the word"—the good life of God modeled for us and mediated to us in Jesus. It has the power to transform our character.

Character When the Moment Is On

Remember the movie *The Karate Kid*? It reveals some all-time great lessons about working on the inner self. The story opens as a teenager, Daniel, is bullied in his new neighborhood. Tired of this treatment and hoping to defend himself, he tracks down Mr. Miyagi at his home and pesters the old master for karate lessons. Mr. Miyagi agrees, but on the condition that Daniel will never question his methods. Then, Mr. Miyagi gives him a series of menial chores:

» Daniel-san . . . come out to the driveway and wax the car: wax-on . . . wax-off.

» Daniel-san, come in the house now and sand the wooden floor: using just this particular circular motion.

» Daniel-san, come out to the backyard and paint the fence by employing this exact up-and-down stroke.

At the end of these chores Daniel comes to the conclusion that Mr. Miyagi is using him. Defying Mr. Miyagi's one rule to never challenge his methods, Daniel bitterly complains about the chores.

Mr. Miyagi, looking Daniel in the eye, adopts a fighting stance and responds: "Daniel-san! Defend yourself!" Daniel too strikes a fighting pose. Mr. Miyagi throws a punch at him and Daniel fends off the blow with a "wax off" motion! Mr. Miyagi attempts a kick, and Daniel blocks the kick with a "paint the fence" move. One more attempted punch by Mr. Miyagi is thwarted by a "sand the floor" circular action of Daniel's arm.

In that moment Daniel learned the brilliance of Mr. Miyagi. You grow through hidden, indirect effort. And when the time comes in the meeting room or in a shop floor conversation, you will find yourself—like Daniel—instinctually doing the right thing.[2]

The path to servant leadership can and does happen this way. But you have to take this inner journey of character transformation. You have to put it to the test. No book will give you all you need. The things I or any other author on servant leadership teaches you are self-authenticating. You've got to experience it to believe it.

John's Story

A friend of mine who is a business owner told me this story. Let's call the character in this story John and the company he works for 12GuysTech. And let's say they make football gear. John is a manufacturing engineer, veteran manager, and long-term employee. He has endured and survived many management fads during his career. His experience has taught him that if he appears to cooperate with the newest trend to come from the vice president's Hawaiian seminar, it will soon go away.

With his typical good attitude (married to his hard-won wariness) John attended his company's new servant leadership training classes. Thinking that servant leadership might have staying power—but remaining a little cynical about it actually working at a corporation—John decided to test servant leadership at home.

John made this vow on a Friday afternoon. That weekend his wife was to be away, and John would be at home with the teenage kids. *Perfect*, he thought, *I'll try serving my teenagers. Dads never impress their teenagers. If I can get their attention through servant leadership, work should be a piece of cake!*

John walked in the front door and jumped into full servant leader mode, saying to the kids: "Hey, I'm going to the store, can I get you anything?" The kids looked confused and replied, "Uh, no, Dad. We're okay." But John was not to be so easily deterred. Later, overhearing hassles about transportation, John popped his head in a bedroom and asked, "Can

I give your friend a ride home?" "What do you *want*, Dad?" His son replied. "Nothing," John answered, "just trying to learn to serve others and to note the effect it has."

John stuck to this attitude and behavior over the course of the weekend, and his kids began to wonder if this was for real. John noticed a deeper connection with his kids, which he knew was genuine. Back at work Monday morning, sitting in a management meeting, John recounted his weekend. With obvious joy, he told his colleagues how serving his kids had renovated his relationship with them.

John was sold. Dropping positional models of leadership (rooted merely in hierarchies and the power they assume) with his kids gave him a glimpse of what he always wanted: love-based influence in their lives. John's story illustrates how servant leadership is self-authenticating.

Bob's Story

As you might guess, not everyone who tries servant leadership becomes a convert. A number of years ago, while first getting acquainted with servant leadership, I asked the owner of 12GuysTech to give me an example of an employee for whom servant leadership failed. He responded,

> I worked with an executive, who we'll call Bob, who resisted servant leadership. I couldn't even crack open the door to his heart or brain. I liked Bob. He was hired because he was uncommonly smart and had a fantastic résumé that demonstrated a clear ability to get real results. But he opposed me on servant leadership for what were to him solid reasons rooted in the management theory he was committed to. Bob had been trained in a positional model of leadership at the larger corporations he had

worked for. By the time he joined my company, servant leadership was already underway. We had an ever-solidifying corporate culture around servant leadership attitudes and practices.

Bob proved once again in our setting that he could get the numbers we needed and was able to deliver on any reasonable metric. But his manner and methods of getting results were a real problem. My insistence on servant leadership was frustrating and confusing to him. One day—with a mix of respect and irritation—he asked me, "Why is my leadership style not accepted here? If I am achieving my quarterly deliverables, why do you care about how I get them?"

Neither of us could have seen it coming. But in that moment I found myself saying out loud for the first time something deep in my heart. "Bob," I answered, "How you get your work done is the only thing I care about."

This story, especially the final sentence, was a turning point for me, causing me to deepen my resolve to become the most effective servant leader possible.

But a deep and solid commitment to servant leadership is not easy to come by. Most of us have been taught overtly and indirectly that quarterly numbers are what count in the rough and tumble business world. People and the rest of life's issues can be ignored, if not damned. Many companies get results by beating up people to deliver results as measured by a given metric. I've seen the carnage from this approach. When we use the positional power model, over time people no longer look out for what is good for the company. They merely duck and cover on their way to the biggest paycheck they can get. The positional model of leadership too often devolves into rewarding the corrupt covetousness of employees by manipulating them with promotions, titles, and money.

My friend continued his story.

> Because I sincerely liked Bob and admired his many strengths, I was sad to let him go. 12GuysTech avoids employee turnover. It is the biggest hidden cost in any business or nonprofit. In the vast majority of cases, adopting servant-led models is the best way to keep good people. Folks like working for honorable managers. But in the end, Bob was one of the few who couldn't make it in our servant-led culture. He was wed to the positional model, to his manner of doing things, and getting results his own way.

Before we finished our lunch conversation about Bob, my friend had one last thing to say.

> Let me brag a bit more about servant-led environments. Even when we lose with an employee, we lose in the most gracious way possible. Bob came back a year later to see me. He came into my office to thank me for all I did to try to make things work out. I don't know if he was softening toward servant leadership or not, but in that moment I was joyful knowing I had served him the best I knew how. Because others in the company witnessed Bob's and my interactions, his apparent loss was actually a win for our culture. It gave people confidence that in tough situations they too would be treated with love and respect.

Next Steps for Servant Leaders

Think about it (reflection). Our character is composed of the mental, moral, and emotional qualities that make each of us distinct. We might think of character as our truest nature.

What in your character is most easily and organically in line with the values and practices of servant leadership? How might you leverage that trait in the cause of servant leadership? What character trait of yours is most inconsistent with servant leadership?

Try it (action/application). Find a few moments to put your best character trait to use in the cause of servant leadership. Are you naturally honest? Find appropriate ways to tell a hard truth that others stuff down, one that is good for the company. Are you willing to do unpleasant chores that make a real difference, but most others avoid? Purposely do a couple of those chores in the next few days.

Evaluate the results (assessment). Notice how others react to you. Were they irritated that you rocked the boat? Did they seem to respect your honesty or selfless work? How did you feel yourself: fearful, but willing to do the right thing? Happy to serve your company, employees, and customers by lovingly using the truth? You could also do the same experiment employing the character trait that is most out of phase with servant leadership.

5

Meeting Demands

> People want to believe you are sincerely interested in *them* as persons, not just what they can do for you. You can't fake it. If you don't mean it, they know it—just as you'd know if someone were pretending to be interested in you.
>
> John Wooden, *Wooden:*
> *A Lifetime of Observations and*
> *Reflections On and Off the Court*

Bob Dylan said it well:

> You may be an ambassador to England or France
> You may like to gamble, you might like to dance . . .
> But you're gonna have to serve somebody.[1]

That is the first question every would-be servant leader has to ask: Who am I going to serve: God, others, or myself? Will I only care about the work and myself, or will I care about those entrusted to my care? My biggest leadership regrets, by far, are those times when I failed to understand, love, and care well for others.

With many years of closely considered hindsight, I know that those moments of hurting rather that serving others came from fear and self-centeredness, from the times when the demands of the job got too high, too tough, or too unpleasant. I then rationalized inappropriate ways of dealing with it. The thought process went something like this:

» If I stay in this situation I might lose some autonomy. I might get hurt.

» This job is not what I thought I signed up for.

» Another group of people would not be so hard to work with.

» Another setting would use my gifts better.

These thoughts *could* be real and valid. But for me they were ways of rationalizing a decision that unnecessarily hurt people. In fear of the future, I left a group of good friends and long-time colleagues feeling abandoned and uncared for. Feeling used in a situation I did not sign up for, I rationalized getting as far away as possible, which destabilized various aspects of my life.

Servant leaders think differently:

» How can I hang in here and do what is right?

» Now that things have changed, how can I serve this new situation?

» How can I lead these people to a new way of being, a new way of working together?

» How can I use my gifts in fresh ways, thereby breathing fresh life into this team?

Over the course of my career, selfish, nonservant thinking has led to frequent bouts of vocational wanderlust. I surmised that the grass would be greener somewhere else. I assumed that a new work setting would fulfill the needs of my ego, and pride. I hoped a new job would better facilitate my neurotic need to matter, to make a difference, and to count for something. Discovering this was a window into my soul, which led to my need for servant leadership.

There is no clear pattern or set of reasons why people don't adopt the attitudes and practices of servant leadership. The human heart is too complex for that. But there are two common hindrances to giving servant leadership a shot: fear and ego.

Control freaks have a hard time letting go and trusting others, core practices in servant leadership. They have trouble with this because of fear. Fear gives birth to controlling attitudes and behaviors. People who live in fear feel compelled to remain tightly in control of everything. They attempt to control themselves and their world.[2]

Fear is a very bad master. Why do we give in to it so easily? What has it ever done for us? It seems that trust and love would pay much bigger dividends!

Trust and love involve *risk*. But don't kid yourself: *we risk much more by being indiscriminate fear-based control freaks.* We risk losing self-esteem, the respect of others, and the possibility of long-term relationships. In business we also risk the costliest thing of all: frequent and wide-ranging employee turnover.

Being a control freak takes no real courage. It is simply a way to give in to and cover up fear. The courageous leader, the one who takes the biggest risks, achieves the greatest successes, and enjoys the biggest rewards, has the audacity to surrender herself or himself to the God-given talents and potential in others. This kind of leader creates a corporate culture that radiates childlike joy at finding new products, creating better services, and discovering more effective ways to conduct business.

I started cleaning pools and mowing lawns in elementary school. I had my first real job at sixteen years old and have had bosses, boards, or some sort of leadership around or over me for forty years now. I don't know how many times I've heard a boss yell, "Why the hell am I always the last one to know anything around here?" "Well, duh," I want to say. "You're the worst listener I've ever known! All you do is blame others! You put the 'ish' in *punish* the messenger!" This kind of boss thinks he or she is being hard-nosed, macho or tough. But in truth this kind of boss is operating out of profound, anxious fear.

Such leaders would be shocked to hear this and would strenuously disagree. Fear is deep-seated and often subconscious. In our work to become servant leaders, and especially by working through the exercises at the end of each chapter, we have tried to expose our truest hearts to the daylight in order to examine and work on them. We do this because as David Benner says in his book *Surrender to Love*, "self-deceptions and an absence of real vulnerability block any meaningful transformation."[3] As servant leaders, we need the transformation of our inner selves.

Fighting Fear with Love

But let's get real here. Most of us hate vulnerability. We see it as weakness, as being soft. And no one, we surmise, can make it in today's marketplace if they are weak or soft. But what if vulnerability is not the path to spinelessness but the road to power?

We hate vulnerability and trusting others in ways that involve the possibility of failure. Why? Because we are self-centered. But if we can break out of this egocentric fear, we will find something fresh, better, and stunningly powerful: the transformation of our leadership. This transformation is worth the effort and has whole-life implications. As author David Benner writes, the "bondage of the self is always the enemy of genuinely self-surrendering and self-transcending love."[4]

This love is the unexpected power I mentioned earlier. Employees respond to love. Customers are drawn to environments, products, and services marked by love. By *love* I don't mean mushy platitudes but *the power of caring for others*. However, we can't get there as leaders or lead our corporate culture there if we insist on *me* as the basic point of reference for our common work. Author David Benner states, "Ultimately, taking care of Number One takes care of no one."[5]

Thus, betting on love actually aligns us with the most fundamental reality of all creation: God. Love will transform the self created by years of fear-based, power-oriented, untrusting leadership, management, and supervision.

Few people know more about leaders' hearts and inner drivers than Henry Cloud, who is a psychologist, consultant, and mentor to hundreds of senior leaders in many work settings. Cloud says, "Who a person is will ultimately determine if their brains, talents, competencies, energy, effort, deal-making abilities, and opportunities succeed."[6]

At my high school, some of the best athletes ruined their potential professional careers by abusing drugs and alcohol. They were stronger, faster, and more gifted than I was. I had to work hard to accomplish the things that came naturally to them. But something in their inner lives sabotaged their potential.

Several of the most talented and gifted people I have worked with eventually crashed and burned. They destroyed their careers through sexually inappropriate behaviors, substance abuse, dishonesty, or mistreating people, leaving thousands of people to wonder whether they could trust God, the church, or religion again.

Cloud offers great insight into servant leadership: "Character equals the ability to meet the demands of reality."[7] But how do we remain secure and able to execute in a setting that is threatening us with hard truths—with *frightening* realities? Is there a way to be present to tense circumstances when our adrenaline is screaming at us to fight or flee? Are we simply our DNA? Just flesh, bones, and water? Are we at the mercy of our body chemistry? Or is it possible that the unseen, invisible, mysterious part of us called *character* rules over matter, over the material world, over our nerves and bad memories?

Yes. Yes it does.

Worry and Anxiety

Leaders who are not truly present to reality cannot serve. They are *not there* in the sense that they are blinded to what is real by fear or anger, maybe even panic. To be dependable servant leaders we need to be a consistent, nonanxious presence in the reality of our day-to-day, moment-by-moment lives. A servant leader must find a way to be safe—to be secure inside him- or herself—not unduly moved by the anxious reactions of others. We can do this as followers of Jesus.

If you can't develop nonanxious leadership, you won't be able to perform as a servant leader in the heat of the moment. Some women and some men embrace the fearful heat; they find ways to make it work nonanxiously in their favor. Reality brings out the best in them.

Maybe you've heard pro golfers say they make truly important putts more often when they putt as if they don't care whether the ball goes in the hole or not. Worry about future consequences and anxiety about what people might think or say are terrible masters. Ditch them. You'll be most loving, offer your finest service, and get the most consistent results for your organization when you focus peacefully on reality.

Reality and Servant Leadership

Being peacefully and appropriately present to reality—to the way things really are—is not heroic. Some leaders are naturally courageous. They relish confrontation and don't mind tough or awkward moments. But being present to reality as a leader is not merely related to your temperament or personality. Being present to your life requires both a shift in perspective and acquiring a new set of skills. As Cloud tells us, "Reality is always your friend. . . . Everything else is a fantasy."[8]

Servant leaders know that leadership happens only in the context of what is real today: the present moment or this quarter's revenues, profits, and share prices. Servant leaders radiate this approach: "I don't care what the truth is, just give it to me. I have to know what is real. Then I can know what to do."[9] Everything else is make-believe. Reality is alive, teeming with possibility: "The world as it really is . . . is where profits are made. The people who see the truth are the ones who always score."[10] Reality is where new products are developed and improved services are conceived. If you are interested in becoming a servant leader, then reality is your friend, your path to effective and ethical servant leadership.

Not Necessarily Nice

Servant leadership is not about being nice. Servant leaders still *lead*. And in any work setting, some people resist being led. That is the way it is. That's reality. Even Jesus, my hero servant leader, did not make everyone happy or leave everyone thinking he was *nice*.

He confronted one guy about his attachment to riches. The man walked away sad (Mark 10:17-22). The leaders who were selling religious necessities and doing currency exchange in a place that was dedicated to prayer found out that Jesus could be a passionate and visionary leader (Matthew 21:12). Jesus wasn't "nice." He could and would clean house, over-turning things (so to speak!) when it was the right and honor-able course of action.

A Riddle

How can I be nonanxious and self-differentiated, so my worth does not depend on what others think of me? How can I lead with integrity? How can I gain the trust of those I lead? You might respond: Is it possible to be truly me and be nonanxious about it? Don't I have to choose one or the other? If I am self-differentiated, won't that create blowback? Won't some people perceive me as arrogant or a loner?

I wish I had read *A Failure of Nerve* by Edwin Friedman when I was a rookie leader in the 1970s. I would have been a more effective leader, made fewer mistakes, and hurt fewer people. Friedman's work on nonanxious self-differentiation is crucial to servant leadership. That being the case, I want to share the following ideas from him:

> Differentiation is the lifelong process of . . . self-definition and self-regulation. . . .

> Differentiation means the capacity to become oneself out of one's self, with minimum reactivity to the positions or reactivity of others.

> [A non-anxious person is] someone who has clarity about his or her own life goals, and, therefore, someone who is less likely to become lost in the anxious emotional processes swirling about. . . .

> [A nonanxious person] is someone who can [self-define] while still remaining connected [to others], and therefore can maintain a modifying, non-anxious, and sometimes challenging [leadership] presence. . . .

> [Such a person] is . . . therefore be able to take stands at the risk of displeasure in others.[11]

If this is your introduction to Freidman, let me link his brilliance to servant leadership for you:

Self-definition. Most of the momentum and expectations

of the marketplace—given its ever-increasing need for profit, and for hitting key metrics with ever-increasing speed (and with ever-decreasing budgets) works against servant leadership. At a minimum these workplace forces make servant leadership counterintuitive. Thus the big takeaway from Friedman: even if you get lucky and your place of work adopts servant leadership principles, *no one is going to make you into a servant leader.* You, from the deepest convictions of your heart, must begin to define yourself in this way. Then you must live into that new way of being in the world.

Don't react to the reactions of others. As soon as you make the heart move to servant leadership, and as soon as others can see your change of heart, you will get pushback. What are you going to do when those inevitable moments come? While caring *for* others, you cannot care *what they think* about your decision to become a servant leader—on that level you need to be unmoved by inner anxiety. This does not mean being cocky, cold, uncaring, or indifferent. Quite to the contrary, taking your stand can be a powerful act of serving, of self-giving love. The right thing can seem to be the hard or wrong thing to do, and the wrong thing can seem right. For instance, imagine that while you are on a small aircraft, the pilot becomes incapacitated. Even though you have never been near the controls of an airplane, you are called to the cockpit to take over. You are given commands. They seem wrong to you. All your inclinations and intuitions say to do the opposite. You are now reacting negatively to the confident self-expression of a veteran pilot. You are a bundle of negative, fearful emotion.

What is the loving thing for the instructor to do? Seeing that you are upset, should she back down? Would that be love? No, loving, servant leadership would not react to you, but maintain her self-definition as the expert. The instructor needs to remain a nonanxious leader. She knows her instructions are the loving thing to do for everyone on the plane and those who could be hurt on the ground. From this knowledge the instructor insists you do as commanded. As a growing servant leader, you want to become as expert, humble, and nonanxious in your servant leadership as a veteran pilot.

Self-differentiate but stay connected. To be self-differentiated while staying connected to your colleagues may seem to be a confusing, even impossible notion. For instance, you might wonder, *Don't I have to remove myself from others in order to find myself, my true self? If I stay connected to others won't that mean they will have some influence on me, thus eroding my capacity to be my truest self?* Let's get at this for a moment. What will be gained in the workplace if you find a new, true *you* as servant leader if you cannot stay connected to those you lead, as well as those who think your newfound style of leadership is stupid, weak, and ineffective? You have to do both. Fully differentiate the best you can, but stay nonanxiously connected to others, even to those who become fearful or angry. A fully self-differentiated, nonanxious presence is the power that gives servant leaders the ability to *modify*, as Friedman says, their team meetings and hallway conversations—in fact their whole corporate culture.

Self-differentiation also has a spiritual dimension. It is virtually impossible to be self-differentiated apart from a healthy relationship with God. Unfailing confidence in God's presence in the life of the self-differentiated individual facilitates the risk-taking inherent in servant leadership.

This is what Jesus meant when he said, "Whoever loses

their life for my sake will find it" (Matthew 10:39). If self-differentiation is a healthy, detached response to possessions, relationships, and all that characterizes the material world, then it stands in the forefront of servant leadership.

Discipline

To pursue personal growth we need a vision. Something outside of us. A better future has to beckon us both *to* it and *through* the aches and pains, frustrations, and setbacks associated with seeking progress in the inner person. When we have a compelling vision, what comes next may not seem sexy or glamorous, but it is core. We must be disciplined. Discipline can't be faked. It can't be forced. It is not drudgery, at least not for a person pursuing a vision.

As a boy I pursued athletic achievement. I practiced basketball in the lighted driveway until late into the night. My mom would threaten and yell until I came into the house and went to bed. My focus on improvement was rooted in a powerful vision of athletic competence. That focus was like blinders on a horse eliminating anything peripheral—like schoolwork, chores, or even other non-athletic things I might have chosen for fun.

Why did I work so hard in sports? I wanted to perform well. I wanted a given skill—such as shooting free throws—to come naturally. I didn't want to be thinking about shooting technique when the outcome of the game was on the line. I wanted to simply shoot: shoot the right way because the right way was ingrained in my muscle memory.

Discipline is our friend. Discipline is like a hero in a movie rescuing us from inability, from anchors that hold us in place when we want to move forward. Discipline grants us the freedom found in the capacity, in the capability to be, move, and do. *We are disciplined when we are the kind of people who can and would do what needs to be done the moment it needs to be done.*

Athletes cherish this capability. Singers and actors would never dream of getting on stage without it. Teachers go to great lengths to be prepared in class. No cop would hit the street without first knowing his or her stuff. No firefighters would be allowed on the scene of a fire without first disciplining themselves physically and mentally. And you cannot show up on the shop floor, conference room, or hallways of your workplace and be a servant leader until you have disciplined your heart, mind, soul, and will.

Are you unconvinced of the rightness or goodness of servant leadership? Is the vision of its powerful, healing affect on humans still a bit fuzzy? Maybe it doesn't seem worth the effort. The only thing that matters in this moment is being real, gut-level honest. If you can see the vision, it will naturally pull you into the heart work you need. It may seem far-fetched to you right now, but it is possible to experience this personal growth in a way that brings you childlike joy, similar to the pleasure I felt shooting baskets in my driveway.

To achieve servant leadership with a modicum of child-like joy requires us to do certain things and avoid others. We'll unpack these in chapter six.

Next Steps for Servant Leaders

Think about it (reflection). Discipline is an uncertain word to many people. It also raises the question: How do I become disciplined? First, let's understand what we are shooting for: A disciplined servant leader has the ability to do what reality calls for in the moment it calls. But, let's also think more about how one engages in various disciplines to become that kind of person. Similar to my basketball story, have you ever, out of loving passion, given yourself to becoming good at something? If so, you were, consciously or not, disciplining yourself and thus becoming the kind of person who could meet the demands of the reality you were practicing for. How does this apply to the kind of growth we are discussing here? For instance, how does someone discipline him- or herself away from anxiety, fear, or worry?

Try it (action/application). Let's say your issue is that you are anxious most of the time. The next time anxiety comes upon you, before you decide to act or not, ask yourself why you are afraid. Be honest. This process will lead you to what you need to work on. You will find that the anxious feelings are often the symptom of a more substantive underlying issue. Maybe you will discover that you cannot stand the thought of disapproval by colleagues. Okay, but why? Maybe you realize that growing up you consistently felt disapproval from your older siblings. Okay, what are you going to do about that? This is the process of spiritual formation that servant leaders need. It can get complex, so it would be great to have a friend or coach to talk with about this. That, in fact, is your next action: pick one of these inner tormentors (e.g., fear, anxiety, anger) and have some conversations about it with someone you trust. Tell this person what you are tying to do (become a servant leader), what holds you back (self-conscious anxiety), and how you learned to engage the world in this way (belittling from siblings). In this, you are looking for modest gains: some self-understanding that becomes a rationale for alternative attitudes and behaviors. For instance: I am more than what my siblings recognized; the "more" that I am can be put to use toward becoming a servant leader.

Evaluate the results (assessment). How did you feel during these conversations? What self-awareness did you gain? How can you turn what you learned into modest forms of action that build confidence in your ability to be a servant leader?

6

Heart Trouble

The Son of Man did not come to
be served, but to serve.

Mark 10:45

"You are just dogs pulling my sled. If you don't like it, if you don't agree with what I am doing, there are plenty of other dogs ready and willing to take your place!" Surrounded by a dozen or so of my colleagues, I sat in the meeting stunned. That is not an overstatement. Never had I heard a leader be so bold. But it wasn't just bold. It demeaned a group of senior leaders who had helped this man build an international enterprise. Sure, he was the star, and maybe other "dogs" could have done as well as we did, but we had been with him, struggling through many ups and downs.

I knew this man well. I loved him before the incident, after it, and up to today. And of course that one moment of bad judgment does not fully define him. But that incident has stuck with me for thirty years as a paradigm of bullying others when you cannot win the argument any other way. It stands the test of time as a model moment when, to get his way, a leader appeals to sheer power rooted in his position in the organization. I'm sure you've seen it too: threats to fire people, dock their pay, or block promotions.

Here is an irony of global proportions: some of the greatest evil ever perpetrated on earth was done in the name of doing good. Think about *religion*. Or *progress*.

Leadership rooted in positional power that is willing to do anything is similarly scary. The scenario often unfolds like this: a person decides that he—and often a team or group of accompanying crusaders—*must* do whatever it takes to implement his vision. "I must get this company turned around," a leader says. Or a coach decides, "We must win more games this year." So far, so good. There is nothing wrong with winning more games or doing better business.

Here is where it goes wrong, letting loose all manner of hurt, dysfunction, cheating, and even evil: "I will do anything— whatever it takes—to get it done!"

Do whatever it takes. This phrase is one of the most troubling and frightening in our language. It pushes a button that unleashes hell on the earth: in friendships, marriages, neighborhoods, and the workplace. When someone is willing to *do whatever it takes* to get something done, the environment becomes toxic.

This doesn't mean we shouldn't work hard to see things through. Obviously, there are times when we have to go the extra mile. But these times should always be temporary. When they aren't, we unleash malevolent forces in our bodies, minds, souls, and spirits. We experience lack of sleep, overexertion, and burnout. Hospital emergency rooms and countless therapists are witnesses to how we harm ourselves with such wrongheaded inner vows.

When someone utters, "I'm willing to do whatever it takes," what is the state of his or her heart? Selfishness? Narrow and short-term thinking? Perhaps greed or grandstanding? Meanness would be there. No one can willingly harm others or turn a blind eye to injury without the antithesis of love—which is contempt—ruling their heart. Contempt for others manifests itself in meanness, unkindness, hatred, cruelty, or heartlessness.

Contempt or meanness (the willingness to harm other for *the cause*) will grow only in certain soil. Right? Some plants are acid-loving, such as gardenias and azaleas. They will only grow in acidic soil, so we buy soil amendments in order to grow beautiful flowers. Other plants, like many evergreens, will only grow in alkaline soil. We adjust the soil according to what we are growing.

Meanness too will grow only in certain types of soil. What is the heart soil that facilitates unthinking, automatic meanness? First, I know that almost no one is intentionally mean. It is hard to imagine a leader rolling out of bed in the morning, saying to herself: "I know what I'll do! I'll be a jerk today." No, what happens is that the *end* seduces and deceives us. The importance of what we are trying to do justifies any means. *I'm willing to do whatever it takes.*

Our twisted hearts—the soil—dictate what comes out of our mouths before we can consciously stop the words. Jesus was unequivocal that "What comes out of the mouth gets its start in the heart. It's from the heart that we vomit up evil arguments, murders, adulteries, fornications, thefts, lies, and cussing. That's what pollutes" (Matthew 15:18 *The Message*).

Pause here to remember the other places Jesus illustrated the truth of outward, visible actions and words coming from what is inside us: trees produce the fruit inspired by their inner DNA; tombs cleaned on the outside leave the inner "reality" dead. Jesus exposes what is most real about the human condition and describes the way forward for would-be servant leaders: "First clean the inside of the cup and dish, and then the outside also will be clean" (Matthew 23:25-26).

These vivid observations of Jesus are invaluable to those seeking the heart of a servant leader. For it is our deep, subconscious motivations that leak anger, contempt, or hatred under pressure. These are the motivations for *doing whatever it takes* to stop someone who is getting in our way or thwarting our will.

Another maladjustment of the heart is the willingness to harm others *for the sake of the cause.* But what flows from a heart bent toward love, to willing the good of others best we can? Is it possible in our workplaces, which are often marked with pragmatically driven ruthlessness, to lead in love? Yes.

There are several things you *can't* do if you lead in love. You can't try to win all the time. You can't manipulate people. And you can't be a power grabber. Let's look at the following examples.

You Can't Try to Win All the Time

Striving to win dehumanizes others. If you succeed, it will have certainly have an unintended consequence: you will have made everyone around you a loser. Do you really want to work with a team who thinks of themselves of losers?

I suggest you carry a thought that has been effective for me in many different leadership settings: Everything is *personal.* So treat everything like it is.

Imagine this. You are called to the boss's office. He asks you to have a seat. Then he says, "Look, this is not personal . . ." You know what comes next: something deeply personal, right? Is it possible to be *impersonally* laid off or told the promotion was given to someone else? What your boss meant was: This is a systemic or cash-flow issue, not *personal* to you. But the best servant leaders, acting from a heart of love, know everything is personal. When you walk into the office of a mature servant leader—one who thinks of others first—you will hear something like this: "I am really sorry. I know this will affect you in important personal ways. But we have to let you go. We will do all we can to serve you in the transition."

You Cannot Manipulate People—Ever!

The boomerang is used for hunting, sporting, and entertainment purposes. You throw it—it comes back to you. The boomerang also illustrates the folly of manipulating one's peers, bosses, or subordinates. What you do to them will come back to hurt your enterprise and haunt you.

Over the last fifteen years I have noticed that many intelligent, capable young women and men steer away from leadership. This is true even when they have visions for teaching, creating new products or services, or combating injustice. Why? They are afraid that it is impossible to simultaneously be an *effective* and *ethical* leader. They presume that a person must be either a manipulative jerk who gets stuff done or an ethical person who gets little done. There is a *tension*, you might say, over *intentionality*.

Let's unpack this and break that rigid, anxious thinking. We can start by defining key words:

> » *Tension.* A state of psychological unrest and stress, or of latent hostility or opposition

» *Intention.* The determination to act in a certain way, to aim at a target; the resolve or will to bring something into being; to focus one's capacity to choose on an object or course of action

» *Manipulation.* To control or play upon another by artful, unfair, or insidious means, especially to one's own advantage; in dealing with people, to give them an appearance of, but not a real, choice in a matter and to do so for selfish interests

Can you see how young potential leaders would be confused? Most of them have known only parents, teachers, coaches, and bosses who got their intended way via manipulation. This leads to the tension over intentionality.

But being *non-manipulative* does not mean being *unintentional.* There are many ways of being ethically intentional. Using Jesus as a model, as we have been in this book, do you think he was consciously intentional about what he was doing? Of course. Did he ever deal unethically with anyone? No. We cannot live unintentionally in any important area of life. And despite social media postings to the contrary, no one is now doing so. Those talking the loudest about "mere relationships" or "mere community" are actually envisioning and intending a course of action as well. They intend an absence of something.

Stuff must be done, action must be taken, decisions must be made to implement any vision. It is like wanting a garbage-free room in the house. Action is required. We must pick up the mess in order to free the room of trash.

Putting this in biblical terms, God did not, after creating Adam and Eve, say, "Now go and merely relate. Have community with each other and with me." Sometimes we think of work and its associated intentionality as a part of the curse. But it is not so. God told Adam and Eve something like this:

> Come, work with me. Be my co-laborers, my subcontractors in this cool new creation I have started. It will be utterly satisfying to you; it is what you are made for. And in the process of doing stuff together you, the human community, and I will develop genuine, nonutilitarian relationships. Instead of feeling used, you will feel like an accomplished artist, dancer, or musician who finally got to Carnegie Hall with your best friends. You then can express this loving relationship for the sake of others in your various places of work.

The invitation to work with God is the greatest invitation anyone will ever receive. In addition, working with God naturally includes intention and purpose. It gives such confidence that we do not need to resort to leadership malpractice to get things done. When working with young leaders, I find that a good way to help them past their cynical fear is to assure them—and this must be genuine—that I do not want things *from* them; I want things *for* them. They will always be free to pursue the course that seems best. Such an attitude, and the actions that naturally spring forth from it, can be a basis for removing the tension from intentionality and becoming a fine servant leader.

Power Grabbing Doesn't Work

You cannot grab power as a basis for leadership leverage. It pollutes servant leadership from the outset. It creates untrustworthy leaders, puts a political spin on things, and fosters a partisan corporate culture. When leaders amass power, some people are used and others are targets. No one likes being either.

Think of the genius of Jesus's servant leadership model. He did not grab power as a means to an end. He lived, without the outward trappings of power, in complete confidence of his calling. At his baptism, before he said a word publicly or accomplished anything for the crowds, he heard his Father say, "This is my Son, whom I love; with him I am well pleased" (Matthew 3:17). We receive a similar affirmation when we hear and positively respond to the creation and covenant call to "Come, work with me. Be my cooperative friends."

That would give a person confidence, wouldn't it? It gave Jesus the poise and ease of character to be the world's greatest servant leader. He always knew he was safe, but not as we might think of *safe*. When he was arrested, he chose not to use his power to overwhelm his captors. When he was unfairly tried before judges, he did not respond with might. Most poignantly, when nailed to a cross, he let evil do its worst to him, knowing that in so doing evil would exhaust its power and one day be defeated forever!

Power to him was not a zero-sum reality. Jesus knew power was in endless supply. He spent most of his time on earth using power to help others and to generously give power to his followers so they too could serve others.

So, how do you put this into practice? Let's look at a few important steps.

The Golden Rule and the Great Commandment

The Golden Rule says, "Do to others what you would have them do to you" (Mathew 7:12). These words, which make up one of Jesus's most famous sayings, should not be relegated to a *saying* in the same category as "I left it all on the field" or "love is blind." The Golden Rule is superb moral wisdom that has anchored the human community in most of the world since Jesus's time. It is not a stretch to say that Western society, when acting at its best, has been built upon it.

Occasionally someone tries to find an exception to Jesus's teaching. However, they almost always misunderstand the context of when Jesus gave the Golden Rule. Jesus was offering a way to both understand and memorize the essential truth of the Old Testament Law and the Prophets. In another setting, Jesus offered a similar summary of Jewish law:

> "Love the Lord your God with all your heart and with all your soul and with all your mind." This is the first and greatest commandment. And the second is like it: "Love your neighbor as yourself." All the Law and the Prophets hang on these two commandments. (Matthew 22:37-40)

In teachings such as the Golden Rule and the Great Commandment, Jesus is not programming robots or making new laws for people to follow. These teachings, though good for anyone to follow, were given to those who intended to follow Jesus. Followers of Jesus are expected to use discernment and prayerfully make the best decisions they can as they implement Jesus's teachings. In my imperfect practice of servant leadership, these two teachings are my go-to, moment-by-moment self-talk. This is particularly the case when I'm preparing for a difficult conversation or a testy meeting.

It really works! Try it for a week. Our minds can process these short sayings in a second or two. Before you pick up the phone for a touchy conversation, ask God to help you to not say or do anything that you would not want said or done to you. Just before turning the doorknob to walk in the meeting room, ask God to fill you with love for your *neighbors* sitting around the table.

Using those two prayers as moment-by-moment guides is a near fail-safe governor on attitude, words, and behavior. But it's not a magic bullet. None of us will be perfect at implementing these magnificent teachings. Just do this: when you fail, review what happened, how you felt, and what you were thinking. Then—without judging yourself harshly—get back to the heart work. If you were really off base, apologize.

"Love your neighbor" and "Do to others what you would have them do to you" are crucial to servant leadership. Here's why: leadership, certainly servant leadership, should be judged not only by the tasks accomplished but by the quality of community it creates in the accomplishing of those tasks.[1]

This means some old but common ways of thinking need to be reframed, or maybe ditched alltogether. For instance, Winston Churchill said, "Healthy citizens are the greatest asset any country can have." Mary Kay Ash observed, "People are definitely a company's greatest asset. It doesn't make any difference whether the product is cars or cosmetics. A company is only as good as the people it keeps." And former CEO of Xerox Anne M. Mulcahy touted, "Employees are a company's greatest asset—they're your competitive advantage." We can agree that these quotes, meant to lift the value of human beings, are worthy of applause. But I want to take the sentiment even further: people (our neighbors in this sense) are not *assets*. Identifying them as such is deneighboring and dehumanizing.

Our coworkers are persons in their own right. The fact that we have an employer-employee relationship with them does not mean they are ours, that we own them. They belong to

God. And even to God they are not *assets*. They are individuals with whom God, as their Creator, has a relationship. In the heart of a servant leader, employees, partners, vendors, bankers, and customers should be prized as Churchill, Kay, and Mulcahy suggest, but even more so. As Madeleine L'Engle wrote: "It seems that more than ever the compulsion today is to identify, to reduce someone to what is on the label. To identify is to control, to limit. To love is to call by name and so open wide the gates of creativity."[2]

How does a would-be servant leader cultivate such a heart for others? Working the Golden Rule and the Great Commandment into your heart and mind will help you prize human beings, develop people, and facilitate community in the workplace. You don't have to be preachy to engage with these principles, to live from them. In fact don't become a self-righteous office nag! Just quietly execute Jesus's insights. People will notice, just as you do when someone cares for you or is fair to you. You are looking for a positive effect on others. You are not trying to win an argument or call attention to yourself.

Which leads me the second thing you must do.

Relax!

When a servant leader in training goes after the heart change I have described, they become capable of leading with relaxed, focused attention. This is what you see in veteran musicians, actors, or athletes. They have trained and prepared so well behind the scenes that once the lights come on they do what is natural to them. This kind of preparation and training happens in the servant leader's inner person: heart, soul, mind, and will.

So far, I have addressed the servant leader's inner life.

Now it's time to look outward to discover how servant leadership is rooted in who watches us lead. Choosing an audience for our leadership is crucial, for it is a key determining factor in how a leader behaves. Should our audience be our families? How about upper management or stockholders? All of those may play some role, but they do not get top billing. That role belongs to someone else. What if you were to conduct your leadership before an audience of one—*the* servant leader Jesus?

Next Steps for Servant Leaders

Think about it (reflection). What do you think of the practice of self-talk? Have you ever tried it? If you stop to think about it, you probably talk to yourself about yourself without conscious thought. It could be negative: *I am so dumb! I can't do this.* I suggest being thoughtful about your self-talk, and talking to yourself in ways that reshape your inner person toward servant leadership.

Try it (action/application). Try talking to yourself for a week. Remind yourself of the Golden Rule, that people are not there for you to use but to serve. As you go through your day (phone calls, meetings, and correspondence), ask yourself, *How do I be a neighbor to this person?*

Evaluate the results (assessment). Did this self-talk feel phony or like you were playacting? Did people respond to you differently? How so? Could you feel your inner self being rewired by your self-talk? Did you feel like the self-talk was echoing the highest inclinations of your heart and driving out disordered desires? If so, what do you make of that?

7

An Audience of One

Character traits supersede gifts,
talents and ability.
Henry Cloud, *Integrity*

S ecrecy. Is it a bad thing? Doesn't the word *secrecy* have undesirable if not immoral connotations? The notion of secrecy often calls to mind clandestine activities and coverups—like the Watergate scandal or tapping the phones of governmental leaders.

But in our context here the practice of secrecy is born from a spiritual motivation rooted in a God-centered worldview. For would-be servant leaders, secrecy is this: in favor of the Divine Audience of One, we abstain from allowing our good deeds and qualities to be known. In secrecy, we cultivate a deep relationship with God that flourishes independent of having to manage the opinions of others by boasting of our goodness, rightness, or power. This is a key discipline in the spiritual formation of servant leaders.

I know of a man who quietly made a huge difference in one of the most intractable racial problems of the twentieth century. He did not tell a soul until it was privately coaxed out of him just before he died. When asked about keeping such an astonishing secret, he explained that he experienced freedom, joy, and power in the discipline of secrecy.

We all know the unpleasant feelings associated with doing something wrong. We run a red light only to see a cop in the rearview mirror. Now filled with regret, fear, or shame, we say things not fit for print. The reverse is true too. Keeping secret our commendable behavior provides a full range of ethical power in our leadership. It brings peace and joy, contentment and satisfaction. I sometimes experience it as an inner *giggle*. I know something others don't: God is working through me, and it is our secret. This inner reality brings poise that radiates to others. Thus the environment around us takes on greater measures of peace, joy, and confidence.

How do we learn the powerful practice of secrecy? By understanding that servant leadership is best practiced within a specific worldview. In simplest terms, a worldview is a set of basic beliefs that become the operating system of a human's life. It refers to a person's fundamental orientation in the world. Our worldview gives us a framework from which we make decisions and a lens through which we view the events and people of our lives.

Managers, supervisors, and leaders typically are not conscious of their worldview. A healthy, workable worldview is not easy to come by. And shifting from one worldview to another takes courage.

The system of values and the principles, standards, and practices that give servant leadership its soul are rooted in a particular worldview. What specific worldview could make servant leadership plausible in the minds of current market-place leaders?

First, servant leadership operates in an open universe, not a closed one. This simply means there are factors at play more powerful and important than the material world of the mar-ketplace or the happiness of shareholders. It means that an outside factor, God, actually cares about this world and its people. There are now a growing number of servant leaders who have seen and can testify that God actually intervenes in and interacts with our world.

Thinking this through liberates us and enables us to operate as servant leaders before an Audience of One. Jesus taught that people should not do good in order to be seen by others, but we should do good to be seen only by God. Jesus said:

> Beware of practicing your righteousness before other people in order to be seen by them, for then you will have no reward from your Father who is in heaven.
>
> Thus, when you give to the needy, sound no trumpet before you, as the hypocrites do in the synagogues and in the streets, that they may be praised by others. Truly, I say to you, they have received their reward. But when you give to the needy, do not let your left hand know what your right hand is doing, so that your giving may be in secret. And your Father who sees in secret will reward you. (Matthew 6:1-4 ESV)

This is not merely a religious or spiritual idea. It is as prac-tical to servant leadership as steel beams are to high-rise office buildings. Living before an Audience of One keeps us from being manipulated or jerked around by the whims, anger, or judgments of others. It gives leaders confidence that enables them to genuinely listen to everyone while remaining true to their own core values.

Being a strong, standup person does not mean being cold, unloving, or a jerk. It calls for meekness, strength, and power under ethical restraint. Meekness is muscular leadership motivated by love. Love, properly understood, means to have the genuine desire in one's heart to do good to others, to never harm. We don't bully. We don't intimidate. We don't mistreat others. Who could do those things with the Audience of One in mind? You wouldn't speed or run a red light with a cop in your rearview mirror, and you won't harm employees when you see them as the creation of God.

Keeping company with the Audience of One in our work also makes us people of peace. It is the only to way to ground ourselves, to feel safe and to secure ourselves in such a way that it eliminates the need to bully, threaten, manipulate, lie, or win. It releases graciousness.

Leading while cognizant of God allows us celebrate, not fear, others. It enables us to give to others from a sense of richness—God's very riches. No zero-sum game here. There aren't winners and losers. It means you believe in the unlimited resources of the One who spoke the world into existence. How is that for a worldview? There is no better theory to undergird and support the heart, attitudes, and behaviors of a servant leader.

Functional Atheism

When we lose sight of the Audience of One, problems often happen something like this: middle management gets pressure from a vice president, who is getting pressure from the CEO. The middle manager begins to pressure employees to "do whatever it takes" to get better numbers on the next report. (On "doing whatever it takes" see chapter six.) I nominate "do whatever it takes" as four of the most devastating and heart-wrenching words expressed in the workplace. They've created heart attacks, strokes, and panic attacks; they've ruined marriages, sent people to prison, and caused parents to abandon children—all because they rationalized the behaviors associated with doing whatever it takes.

This is what Parker Palmer calls *functional atheism*. Functional atheism is "saying pious words about God's presence in our lives but believing, on the contrary, that nothing good is going to happen unless we make it happen."[1] I have observed this godlessness in my own heart and in the lives of many leaders. During the grind of daily business, unbelief may seem insignificant. It actually leads to a destructive mindset. Then, such thinking moves us to supposing and acting as if nothing good is going to happen apart from our own actions. We've all seen this attitude in the halls of commerce, education, politics, or the nonprofit world. Once people get it in their heads that they need to make something happen, well, Katie bar the door, all hell is about to break lose. We've been over that ground—right?

Palmer teaches that functional atheism is triggered by insecurity about our identity and worth. This insecurity inevitably results in believing that leadership is a zero-sum game, that there is a limited amount of power or leadership available in the universe. Then, often because of the law of unintended consequences, we create settings that deprive others of their identities in the senseless fight for power.

There is more power in creation than humans will ever need. Our collective need for power is like the plastic cap of a water bottle. God's provision of power is like Lake Superior—about 32,000 square miles!

Quit fighting. Relax. Believe. Drink from the lake and lead others there so they may drink with you.

Management Theories

I studied business management in college during the mid-seventies. At the time much conversation centered on what motivates people in the workplace and how to best manage people for results. The ideas are out of fashion now, but you might remember Theory X and Theory Y management. Theory X assumes that people would rather not work, especially in a hard and focused manner. They are working only for the money. Thus, workers need to be sat on, controlled, bossed, and highly regulated by countless rules and tight supervision.

In this system, power is king. No one, this theory supposes, works for the good of others (customers, owners, or fellow employees) or for the joy and satisfaction of working.

Theory Y states that people know, and feel deeply in their hearts, that work is good and pleasurable in its own right. Work is as natural as recreation. Theory Y argues that humans are significantly underutilized in the workplace when treated in a Theory X manner, that their innate God-given creativity is squashed to the detriment of the enterprise. Obviously, salaries and paychecks matter to everyone. We need money for rent, car payments, student loans, and food. But it is not the most fundamental human drive. The deepest and most persistent driver of human action in the workplace is the satisfaction that comes from knowing that one has made a difference in and through his or her work.

I found these discussions interesting, but I did not have enough experience to come to a mature conclusion on the matter. In college, I leaned toward Theory Y, but I couldn't have told you why. In hindsight I was probably projecting my love for work and for making a positive difference in the world.

Years later, however, I stumbled across the writing of Max De Pree. Though I've quoted him already, I want to formally introduce you to his writing, especially his books *Leadership Is an Art* and *Leading Without Power*. Every would-be servant leader needs to read De Pree's books, digest the truths in them, and execute those truths in their work.

Hidden Passions, Buried Talents

In *Leadership Is an Art*, De Pree tells a story about his father, the founder of the Herman Miller Furniture Company, attending the funeral of one of his employees, a millwright. The elder De Pree accepted an invitation to the home of the deceased man after the funeral. While he was there, the man's wife asked if she could read some poetry. Who could say no to a grieving widow?

As De Pree listened he was surprised by the delightful poetry. When the woman was done reading, he asked for the name of the poet. He was stunned to hear it was her husband! Walking away from the scene, he began to think: "Was [the dead man] a poet who did millwright's work, or was he a millwright who wrote poetry?"[2]

This story has lodged in my mind for twenty years. How many people in our organizations have hidden passions and buried talents? To what degree are our organizations impoverished and made less effective because we do not really know—or even care to know—our colleagues and employees?

The ancient wisdom of Scripture is the best source of how servant leaders treat others. Proverbs 22:6 says, "Start children off on the way they should go [according to their God-given characteristic, gift, or bent] and even when they are old they will not turn from it." People have a divine bent, a God-given shape. Servant leaders, looking beyond profit to something intrinsically good, try to discern this bent and develop it in order to help the gift flourish. Then the leader can deploy the person according to this bent for the good of the employee and the given enterprise.

Jeremiah 1:5 is even more straightforward about divine design. Before we come to know our colleagues or have any interaction with them, God has already shaped them. God says to Jeremiah, a teenager,

> Before I formed you in the womb I knew you,
> before you were born I set you apart;
> I appointed you as a prophet to the nations.

Well now, this gets us back to the worldview discussion. What do you honestly think about all this? Does God really look after human beings in this way? Does he closely care for and competently love his whole creation? How you answer this question will set the course for your leadership. It simply can be no other way.

If you believe we live in a world in which God fervently loves humans and interacts with them, you will never view people the same way again. Your respect for people will begin to grow in unimaginable ways. As C. S. Lewis wrote,

> There are no *ordinary* people. You have never talked to a mere mortal. Nations, cultures, arts, and civilizations—

these are mortal, and their life is to ours as the life of a gnat. But it is immortals whom we joke with, work with, marry, snub, and exploit—immortal horrors or everlasting splendours.[3]

If you are with me so far, but need just a bit more for the penny to drop, ponder these famous lines from Psalm 139:13-16.

> For you created my inmost being;
>> you knit me together in my mother's womb.

> I praise you because I am fearfully and wonderfully made;
>> your works are wonderful,
>> I know that full well.

> My frame was not hidden from you
>> when I was made in the secret place,
>> when I was woven together in the depths of the earth.

> Your eyes saw my unformed body;
>> all the days ordained for me were written in your book
>> before one of them came to be.

In this picture painted by the psalmist, a servant leader is not someone who, suddenly feeling generous, gives value to others. Rather, from the biblical worldview servant leaders simply and humbly discern something already true: human beings have God-given capabilities and dignity. This inherent value of createdness, of personhood, is not something we can give others. Remember: people are not your *best asset*; they are *human beings* with a life that, coming from a transcendent place, transcends the workplace. This concept should be deeply rooted in the heart of every servant leader.

Servant leaders are convinced that human beings enter the workplace as authentically gifted persons.[4] De Pree says, "One reason servant leaders are so positive in the lives of those they lead—and a key reason they inspire superior work—is that they give the gift of recognition through altruistic listening, observation, trust, and selfless love."[5] The art of servant leadership lies in trusting, polishing, liberating, and enabling the massive potential in the gifts of those we lead, he writes.[6]

This view challenges a strictly legalistic, contractual, utilitarian view of work and relationships, De Pree tells us.[7] It opens the way for something more reciprocal, mutual, and covenantal.[8] A legalistic atmosphere controlled merely by things like rules, job descriptions, and hierarchies of power create environments in which the creative breath of God, as seen in the psalmist, is stifled.

Isn't it amazing that God would give leaders this kind of power? Enough to suppress his divine imprint or to suffocate the noblest impulses of a workforce! But that same power can be put to work with God and his design in others. When we do, we move in the direction of the true nature and potential of servant leadership.

Here I want to make clear the practicality of what I've been saying about the inner, hidden dimension of servant leaders. Discerning the imprint of God on others requires cultivating a quiet, poised, and focused inner being. But it doesn't mean you have to necessarily change your personality. For instance, an effective servant leader doesn't have to be monk-like to adopt the practice of *noticing*. A leader can be a sociable extrovert who also develops the ability to be present to others such that he or she notices what is most real about them.

What is the nature of such leaders? Who would go to the trouble of being present to others, instead of treating others as extras in a movie? What does it take to become an aware and discerning leader? We'll find out in chapter eight.

Next Steps for Servant Leaders

Think about it (reflection). Do you believe God observes our leadership? Do you think he cares about what leaders do? Instead of filling you with guilt, shame, or fear, how could knowing you have a divine audience energize and enliven you as a servant leader? What if God already loves you and is completely committed to you? God is not like the policeman in the rearview mirror; he is the smiling mom or dad helping you learn to ride a bike.

Try it (action/application). Over the next few days seek to be alert to God watching you as you lead. Pray. Ask him to teach you, give you insight and lead you as you lead others. Silently and unobtrusively carry on a conversation with God about how to serve the best interests of the people you interact with. Don't be self-conscious about it. Have no expectations or judgments; simply experience it for what it is.

Evaluate the results (assessment). What did you experience? Did knowing God was watching free you? Was it like having Dad or Mom cheering you on? Or did it make you nervous and wary of doing wrong? What might your reaction teach you about your view of God?

8

The Nature of Servant Leadership

Who a person is will ultimately
determine if their brains, talents, competencies, energy and
effort . . . will succeed.

Henry Cloud, *Integrity*

"Well, I'm only human!" No truer words have
ever been used to cover more harm. "I'm
only human" is meant to convey the idea
that, given our human nature, "We have limits" or "We can't
do everything" or "We can't be perfect." Fair enough. But
too often today those words are meant to cover almost every
wrong or explain away all patterns of poor behavior.

Here is the deal: of course we are only human. That is not
saying much. There's more: our nature can grow, deepen, and
be transformed. This transformation is what servant leaders

pursue as a first-order issue. In this chapter I want to help you think more deeply about it.

I have coached young leaders during most of my career. I've seen those who can't help but cut people off when they feel threatened, and others who accuse people without knowing all the facts. I've known men who habitually threaten others rather that reason with them. I've worked with women who tell lies to avoid confrontation. Yes, we are only human, but these are not the only human options available to us. Transformation is both possible and needed.

Servant leadership literature assumes that specific characteristics are needed to be a servant leader. These include listening, empathy, healing, awareness persuasion, stewardship, commitment to the growth of others, and building community.[1] But what do we do if our default positions are the opposite: being talkative, self-centered, hurtful, inward, argumentative, and wasteful? Maybe we worry that the success of others harms us. What if, despite our stated values and best efforts, we are still the kinds of leaders who impede community? Humility is a core trait for servant leadership. How do we become humble? Why would someone attempt it? What would cause a responsible leader to pursue an unpretentious manner?

In my experience change comes to those leaders who have seen and placed their confidence in a *reality* that transcends the workplace. Only deep, personal change will suffice. This is why I believe servant leadership requires a change of heart before a change of leadership or management practices is possible.

Jesus and his first followers were having a discussion about who should have the highest places of honor. Jesus said:

You've observed how godless rulers throw their weight around, . . . and when people get a little power how quickly it goes to their heads. It's not going to be that way with you. Whoever wants to be great must become a servant. Whoever wants to be first among you must be your slave. That is what the Son of Man has done: He came to serve, not to be served—and then to give away his life in exchange for many who are held hostage. (Mark 10:42-45 *The Message*)

What is Jesus commending here? Is there something his followers need to do in order to be leaders who serve?

First, one cannot understand Jesus's words without knowing the whole story of the people of God. God called his people to be his servants, ministers, and ambassadors, obeying God with childlike joy in a responsible and interactive relationship. The way of Jesus is subversive; it turns upside down the values and practices normally found in positional or hierarchical power.

Jesus's words point to his death on the cross. This is the highest form of servant leadership exhibited. As one noted biblical scholar has put it:

When we look at the picture [the Gospel] is drawing, we . . . may be amazed, horrified, and afraid. But Jesus is going up to Jerusalem, turning the world's values and power systems on their heads, setting off to give his life a ransom for many. If we want to receive what he has to offer, we have no choice but to follow.[2]

How do we follow Jesus's lead? What does Jesus want of twenty-first-century leaders? Do his first-century, agrarian, pastoral words make sense in our high-tech, intensely busy times? Yes, but they require a difficult, but doable, change of heart and mind.

I know there is pushback against this. Some argue that servant leadership will never be widely practiced because it requires such dramatic change. But what if pursuing this inner change brings the highest meaning in life? What if it is the path not only to being a better boss but a better person?

Humility and Vision

We expect to hear words like *humility* and *meekness* in Bible study, a sermon, or a Sunday school lesson—but at work? Truthfully, those words have not shown up much in my world, and I work around religious people! Nevertheless, though they are not the only traits needed, humility and meekness are core elements of servant leadership. Servant leaders still need to cast vision, define reality, strategize, solve problems, manage cash, find and develop products, and recruit and train personnel. Author Ken Blanchard says that there are two central roles for servant leaders: A *visionary* role, setting the course and the destination, and an *implementation* role, doing things right with a focus on serving.[3] Servant leadership does not set aside any of these tasks.

The tasks outlined by Blanchard represent the *what* of leadership in general. Servant leadership characterizes the *how*. Though leadership involves a set of practices, it must also be spiritual, *coming from the unseen world of our inner selves*. The best leadership theories go deeper than mere personality traits or patterns of behavior to underlying matters of the heart. It is increasingly clear in the marketplace that a leader's spiritual formation or lack thereof is either a source of strength or a weakness, a source of credibility or untrust-worthiness.

Let's take these two heart-illustrative words—*humility* and *meekness*—one at a time and explore what they mean in the context of servant leadership.

Humility

Following Jesus's lead, humility was commended by his first followers as well. For instance, Peter said, "Humble yourselves under God's mighty hand, that he may lift you up in due time" (1 Peter 5:6). Another translation puts Peter's words in the vernacular: "Be content with who you are, and don't put on airs. God's strong hand is on you; he'll promote you at the right time. Live carefree before God; he is most careful with you" (*The Message*).

Humility is the capacity to not make yourself the focus of life. I am, after all, only one of seven billion people on the earth, and they all matter a great deal. You might have expected me to say that humility means to not think too highly of yourself. It can include that, but humility is best understood as the capacity to be self-forgetful, to focus on achieving the best for others.

Dallas Willard speaks of a three-step way to exemplify a humble leader: *Never pretend, never presume, never push.* He unpacks this thought:

> *First, never pretend.* Be yourself. We all face those tight moments when we are tempted to claim inside knowl-edge or special talents we don't possess. Or we make quick promises we know we can't keep. Under pressure we may downplay our abilities because we think it makes us

appear humble. Wrong on all counts. True humility claims nothing more or less than the truth. What you see is what you get.

Second, never presume. So often we think we know what others are feeling or we act as if we can read minds. Humility doesn't pass judgment on why people do what they do or why they say what they say. The humble man realizes he looks on the outward but God alone sees the heart. He refrains from snap judgments, hasty conclusions, and negative assumptions. When he doesn't know, he simply says, "I don't know." We could save ourselves from a ton of worry if we stopped presuming on the future or on what others might do or say.

Third, never push. Humility waits for the Lord to move first. Sometimes we get in trouble because we try to force people to do what we want. This may be expressed by giving commands in a loud voice or by nagging others or by making a series of critical comments or even by using violence to get our own way. If we were asked, we would all say we don't like to be treated that way. People want to be led. They hate to be pushed. They want the freedom to think things through and to come to their own conclusions.[4]

Willard helps us to see that humility is not a religious or churchy idea. Those on the receiving end of it find it healing, empowering, and inspiring, words that every leader would want to have said about them. Subordinates and colleagues who experience humble leadership work harder, smarter, and with more joy and effectiveness.

Meekness

Meekness is not weakness. The attributes of meekness are God-fearing, long-suffering, forgiving, not easily provoked, gentle, and kind. Those are not the traits of a weak person. On the contrary, they are characteristics of a strong, secure, and grounded person. Meekness develops and works only in a Godward heart. There is a basis for the restraint inherent in meekness. It is the knowledge that in every difficult conversation, every challenging meeting, every downturn in the market, every slump in profit margins, and every cash flow crisis, humble and meek trust in God is possible. This trust in God is the all-important third way between doing nothing out of fear and taking control and doing whatever it takes to get our way.

We need to decide: will we, in humility and meekness, trust God, or lead from the twisted inner energy that comes from frustration, bitterness, or anger? It's obvious which attributes of the heart produce servant leadership.

Humility and meekness are not natural to most of us. It can sometimes feel like everything in us is domineering, proud, stubborn, and obstinate. We must cultivate humility and meekness for the fruit of servant leadership to become visible in our lives.

What is the path like to get there? It all begins with a decision.

Next Steps for Servant Leaders

Think about it (reflection). What is your honest gut reaction to the words *meekness* and *humility*? Are they attractive words? Do they give you a vision for beautiful and effective leadership? Or do they seem old-fashioned, out of touch, or unachievable? What in your background or experience might have shaped this attitude? Do you need to rethink it or get a fresh perspective?

Try it (action/application). Try leading today without thinking much about yourself. Think of others. Consider how you might bless a family member without calling attention to yourself. Notice—really notice—someone living on the street. Be grateful for others: pastors, cops, and firefighters, civil leaders, talented and dedicated doctors and teachers. Think of the people in your company or enterprise. Think of your dearest goals and objectives—anything but you!

Evaluate the results (assessment). Did you notice increased focus on the people and issues at hand? Did life seem less distracted? Was your day marked by simplicity, clarity, and straightforwardness?

9

Making the Decision

Teach . . . with your life: by word, by demeanor, by love, by faith, by integrity. . . . Keep a firm grasp on both your character and your teaching. Don't be diverted. Just keep at it. Both you and those who hear you will experience salvation.

1 Timothy 4:12, 16
The Message

To serve should be a privilege, and it is to our shame that we tend to think of it as a burden, something to do if you are not fit for something better or higher.

Madeleine L'Engle,
Walking on Water

We were riding in a rental car, heading back to the airport after teaching together at a conference. I was driving, with my dearest mentor riding along in the passenger seat. At some point there came a breather in our friendly debrief about the conference. Into the silent pause came these words, "Todd, I want to talk you in an avuncular manner." Not wanting to let on that I didn't know what *avuncular* means ("like a loving uncle, especially with kindliness or geniality"), I just nodded my head and said okay.

What followed were words of true love, kindness, and the most genial encouragement that has been given to me. It wasn't sloppy, vacuous sentimentality. He thought I was late beginning the kind of work he thought I should be doing. He was challenging me to drop my well-rehearsed excuses and tightly argued justifications and get started.

This brilliant and godly man has since passed on to his place with God. He was supremely talented, highly accomplished, and usually the smartest person in the room, but what I most remember about him is not the size of his gifts or the impact of his work, but the quality of his love. I reminisce about his humble servant's heart. If he had something important to say, without a hint of social awkwardness or pretense he would take my arm and pull me close, and in a hushed tone convey the deepest insights imaginable. Or seeing me a bit anxious about something, he would reach over and pat my arm to reassure me. Those are the actions of a servant leader, of a world-famous man taking the time to serve a younger leader who had no status of any kind.

Leaders oriented to power and protecting their place in the hierarchy have a much more difficult time acting or speaking like that. "I must not be seen with people who could harm my personal brand." Or "I don't have time to invest in others. I've got to take care of myself; no one else is going to do that!" Or "Expressing that kind of care for someone is scary; it makes me feel vulnerable."

But now it's time to make a decision: what kind of leader do you want to be? This chapter is dedicated to helping you make that decision. You know by now I am an evangelist for servant leadership, and I am going to ask you to enter into its power and beauty.

I speak of servant leadership in terms of *beauty* because beauty creates pleasure, satisfaction, or an increased sense of well-being in the beholder. We need more beauty in our workplaces. Certainly some things in our work can go beyond drudgery. We need beautiful work and servant leadership to cast vision for being agents of good in the world. Elaine Scarry observes,

> The absence of beauty is a profound form of deprivation.
>
> Beauty repeatedly brings us face-to-face with our own powers to create, we know where and how to locate those powers when a situation of injustice calls on us to create.
>
> The beholder, in response to seeing beauty, often seeks to bring new beauty into the world and may be successful in this endeavor.[1]

On the other hand, ugly words and menacing body language almost always provoke scowls and nasty replies. Maybe, like thousands of others, you are deeply frustrated by how you are treated at work, as well as by what you see and hear. Perhaps you feel that important beliefs and values are being compromised.

Thankfully, there is another option available to us besides

saying and doing nothing, or retaliating with the same behavior. This third way is the route by which servant leaders walk, the route of creative good, of being willing to work for and give birth to a new reality, vibe, and culture at work.

In *Walking on Water* Madeleine L'Engle writes, "The artist is the servant who is willing to be a birth-giver. . . . The artist (male or female) like Mary, who, when the angel told her she was to bear the Messiah, was obedient to the command."[2] We are not going to give birth to the Son of God, as Mary did. But we can give birth to his way of being in the world, to his values and his love. Following Christ has nothing to do with success as the world sees success. It has to do with love, L'Engle reminds us.[3] Who can or would want to argue against love, against desiring the best for others and organizing one's inner life around seeking the good of others?

The challenge is that love appears sloppy. Business needs to be quick, clear, and efficient. Willing the good of others seems naive. Fighting for one's slice of the market is an essential definition of commerce. Seeking to change one's inner, hidden, interior life sounds almost monastic against the backdrop of most interactions in the workplace.

As you are thinking about what you'll do next, consider that ethical and effective ways of leading are possible. Though market forces and the social psychology of the workplace can seem fixed, there is hope. We need to reinvigorate our imagination.

For instance, L'Engle further teaches that

In so-called primitive societies there are two words for power, *mana* and *taboo*: the power which creates and the power which destroys; the power which is benign and the power which is malign. Odd that we have retained in our vocabulary the word for dangerous power, *taboo*, and have lost *mana*.[4]

Servant leadership is part of the "mana"—the power that creates. It's not just about being compassionate. It's about being a positive and constructive force for good in the world.

I find the "for the good of others" rationale for servant leadership beautiful, elegant, and persuasive. Thus, I believe servant leadership itself is *beautiful*. I chose that word purposely, for "what is beautiful prompts the mind to move chronologically back in the search for precedents and parallels, to move forward into new acts of creation, to move conceptually over, to bring things into relation, and does all this with a kind of urgency as though one's life depended on it."[5]

Perhaps you wonder if you can really commit to servant leadership? This is a critical decision. The *you* that will emerge in the months and years ahead depends on what you choose. As soon as you decide what to measure, what counts, and what to celebrate, you have set both the trajectory of your career and the basic culture of the enterprise you lead. So what will it be: *positional power motivated by fear, control, and winning driven by zero-sum thinking? Or the path of servant leadership based on a transformed heart of love that desires the good of others?* Perhaps you're not be ready to make this decision. Are you still struggling with the chief pushback against servant leadership: that it is unrealistic, idealistic, or naive?

Let's dig a bit deeper.

Servant leadership worked for Jesus, and he is the unrivaled leader in the history of humanity. No one has influenced the number of people Jesus has. *Well, yes, easy enough for him; he was God, for crying out loud!* you might be thinking. Jesus could do things we can't. That is true. None of us will die for the sins of the world. None of us are going to walk on water or turn water into wine. But the *qualities of being* Jesus taught and tells us are available to his followers—love of neighbor, the Golden Rule, kindness, patience—do not come from divinity but from transformed human hearts. You don't have to be God to embody these qualities. And these characteristics are the inner fountain from which flow attitudes and deeds of servant leadership.

With genuine respect for the great religions of the world, I've nonetheless come to believe that Jesus's way of being in the world, his life, teachings, and death, best explain the most important aspects of human living, including leadership in the workplace.

Who Can Become a Servant Leader?

A person who becomes a servant leader has to be intentional about it. She or he clearly aims to adopt servant leadership as an "easy yoke and light burden," a way of life that brings peace to their soul, harmony to their relationships and goodwill to the culture they create through the exercise of their leadership. Leadership based on amassing power, manipulating people, and fudging the facts is a "hard and heavy yoke" to bear. It leads to broken relationships, ruined partnerships, divorce, addictions, and in many cases the demise of a career.

Jesus contended that ultimate reality is God and his kingdom. He evangelized by asking his hearers to arrange their affairs based on the reality he offered. Jesus knew the power of the human will and our capacity to choose and to set our minds on something.

When offering his listeners a way of life (or for our purposes here, a way of leading) made distinct by his light and easy yoke—Jesus frequently spoke in parables. Jesus's parables were designed to help his hearers grasp what is real. For instance, you may have heard his famous parables about a treasure buried in a field and a pearl of utmost value (Matthew 13:44-46). Jesus told these parables as a way of clarifying our intention regarding the kingdom of God. If we were a real estate entrepreneur and found a field with vast treasure buried in it, would we sell all our assets to get it? Similarly, if we were a pearl merchant and found the pearl of ultimate value, would we sell our storehouse of lesser pearls to get it? Now, think about this: seeing the value of servant leadership to the workplace, are you willing to arrange your heart and leverage your intellectual, emotional, and spiritual assets to become a servant leader?

Jesus told a story of a man who threw a great dinner party and invited many guests. One by one they sent regrets, using various excuses. The man hosting the party then threw open the doors to anyone on the streets who wanted to come (Luke 14:15-24). Jesus invited his hearers to his "banquet." Will you accept his invitation? I invite you to accept it and to experience servant leadership. The first step is up to you.

You can make many excuses to not attend the banquet: the present state of your heart, soul, or thought life; the leadership culture where you work; or the nature of your boss. Will you hear the invitation, accept it, and open yourself to risk and change? It's an invitation to a conversion of sorts that can change the workplace—one leader, one office and one worksite at a time.

The Path to Servant Leadership

The best learning takes place when our experience exceeds our education. The gap between experience and education produces several good things for learning and retention rates.

When I was thirty-five, I attended seminary. I already had sixteen years of experience in ministry. I was motivated to study because I had enough practice in the tasks of ministry to know the gaps in my knowledge.

My biggest takeaway from those three years came from two of my fellow students, both of whom were in their early twenties and straight out of college. In a Greek New Testament class we took together, one of them sat to my right, the other to my left. Greek, the original language of the New Testament, captivated me. In my Sunday sermons I was teaching from the New Testament. Discovering insights into the Greek language made it come alive for me. I could then make the Bible come alive to others. But I frequently overheard my two young friends complaining about what a waste of time it was studying Greek vocabulary and grammar.

Driving away from the campus one day, many years ago, I had a major *aha* moment. I realized that my attitude was different. I didn't enjoy studying Greek because I was a better person than those students, but because of three crucial issues in leadership development:

1. I knew what I didn't know.

2. I knew why I needed to know it.

3. I had an immediate place to apply what I was learning.

When these three realities are not in place, all leadership information, no matter how good it is, no matter how compellingly it is presented, will be theoretical.

In the two decades since that class, I discovered that leadership development happens along parallel tracks. One track is formal education. The other track is experience. The seminary incident taught me that experience ought to outstrip education. When this is the case, motivation to learn and retention rates skyrocket. Leadership development is a blend of information and formation, with a tilt to formation.

What has your leadership or management experience shown you about *what you don't know*? Take a moment to identify some of these things. Because you can't work on several things at one time, especially things of the heart, I suggest you prioritize three of them. Then, put those three in a logical sequence, beginning, as Jesus taught, with inward growth first. If all three are interior issues, then pick the one that has been most on your mind, or the one you see the clearest, or the one you see as most harmful to being a servant leader. Little by little, work on it in inconspicuous ways.

If you need help, find a supportive friend (outside of work if need be) with whom you can be honest about the heart work you are doing. You might also check out the suggested reading list in appendix three.

How Do I Start?

Getting started on the road to servant leadership is simple. Tackle your next acts of leadership as a *servant*. Start with some relatively insignificant acts of leadership. Don't practice it when your company or a key client or important relationship is on the line. Take your time; work slowly but steadily until your new leadership heart feels grounded and confident regarding big issues and key moments.

At the beginning take some small and appropriate risks. Extend some trust to a colleague. Rely on a subordinate's judgment or decision-making ability. Empathize with a coworker who genuinely needs help to grow in his or her job. Think the best of an employee. Give someone the benefit of the doubt. Then monitor your inner self. Were you nervous? Did you feel the immediate impulse to grab power in order to control the outcome? Or did you feel the goodness and appropriateness of servant leadership? Do you notice the effect on others: their smiles, the increased trust they have in you, and the upsurge of motivation to add value to the company without any cajoling? Monitor your feelings and reactions. Step by step learn a new way of being in the workplace.

Once you've begun the process, I recommend that you get a coach. Reach out to the Servant Leadership Institute, which can show you how to implement servant leadership in your workplace and train your key leaders in the principles and practices of servant leadership. You can find information on this at the end of the book.

Coaching is invaluable for a number of reasons, but three are crucial in my experience. Let's take a look at them.

Good Coaching Always Begins with Assessment

Good coaching begins with assessment. If you want to learn to play the piano or throw a baseball, you find someone to assess your talents. A piano teacher would ask you to sit down and play something. The baseball coach might watch you throw the ball. They would both observe and assess your strengths and weaknesses. Apprentice servant leaders need this kind of assessment too. It might not always be fun. It can be frustrating. But deep, long-lasting change requires it.

While in elementary school my mother insisted that I broaden my interests to something other than sports. She suggested piano lessons. I thought it was the least manly thing a young jock could possibly do. She didn't budge, so off I went on Thursday afternoons to the piano teacher.

Because we had a piano in our home, I had plunked around on it. At my first lesson the teacher asked me to play something. She began to comment, based on her expert observations, on my posture, the angle of my wrists, the misuse of the sustain pedal and the way I improperly fingered notes.

As the lessons went on, she was unrelenting in her constructive criticism. Most maddening to me were the times she would send me home with a piece of music to learn. I would do so, come back and play it well, only to have her criticize *the way* I played it. At some point I protested, "What do you mean? I just played the piece right!" Her reply has shaped my coaching and teaching for forty years. "Yes, Todd, you did. But you cannot move on to more difficult pieces using the wrong fingering. You got the notes and the timing right, but you played it the wrong way."

You will have moments like this as you train to be a servant leader. You will have moments when you play the right leadership notes, but with the wrong fingering in your heart. Or you'll be leading in a difficult situation and find that you resort back to old ways of leading. A good coach can talk you through those moments, assisting you in seeing clearly and adjusting your leadership posture.

Good Coaching Employs the Power of Great Questions

Most of us overestimate the power of information. Telling others what to do, or pleading with them to do something, does not compel deep or lasting change. For instance, at five feet, eleven inches tall I used to weigh about 330 pounds. I was seriously round. I shopped in the *big* section of the Big and Tall shop. Friends said things like, "Is that your belt or the equator?" They addressed me playfully as "Your Circumference!"

But calling attention to my girth or describing potential health problems didn't change my eating habits. I was medicating pain with food. I was using food to entertain myself. I was using food to distract myself from anxiety. Those rewards were much more powerful than the information coming from weighing myself on a scale or from the remarks of people who loved me and wanted the best for me.

What finally broke through to me was answering some thoughtful questions put to me by a competent counselor. This gently led me to insights about my relationship to food, and about the inner realities that drove my addiction to it. Mere information usually is not sufficient to produce deep change. Neither is its cousin: pleading for change.

As a young baseball player I had lots of experience with family and friends sitting in the stands behind home plate and loudly encouraging me with comments like, "Come on Todd, watch the ball!" I had heard this so much by the time I was in high school, I wanted to yell back, "What do you think I am doing here? Watching the birds in the sky? Checking out the pitcher's socks?"

I was trying to watch the ball! I needed an insightful coach to *train* me to actually watch the ball. This happened while playing for a great coach in college. He said, "Todd, next time you are up to bat, try to observe which way the red stitches on the ball are spinning." It changed the way I hit the ball.

For facilitating human change, yelling commands like "Watch the ball!" to a baseball player or "Quit being a jerk!" to a boss are seriously ineffective. But coaching questions, such as, "What did you notice about your heart or state of mind when Mr. Rude spoke up at the meeting?" accelerate human transformation.

If you want to get started as a servant leader, find a coach. Coaches of servant leaders do not have to understand your line of business. They don't have to already know you. Once you explain *what you need to know* (what is going wrong or what you are noticing about your inner reactions as a leader), *why you need to know it* (your exchanges with people are not going well), and *how, when, or where you would like to apply new insight* (you can never say what you think in meetings without blurting it out in anger), a coach can guide you toward self-learning so you become your own best teacher.

Self-learning is important for two reasons. First, your coach can't tail you at work all the time. To use the old adage, an effective coach won't merely give you a fish to eat. She will teach you to fish so you can eat for a lifetime. A good coach will help you make adjustments to your feelings, thinking, attitudes, and behavior as you move through the people and events of any given day.

Second, good coaching leaves responsibility where it belongs. You are responsible for being a solid and consistent servant leader; your coach isn't. A coach is like a midwife:

present to help. But you are the mom giving birth to servant leadership. A coach cannot give you the inner desire to change. This has to come from within you.

A coach can't be honest for you. You've got to be candid about the state of your heart and your thinking. A coach can't inject you with love for others. You must cultivate it little by little, day by day. But a talented coach can come alongside to assess you through listening, observing, and asking great questions. This will increase your confidence that you can grow as a servant leader.

Are you ready to try? Or do you have doubts that you can really do it? Let's tackle those doubts, so you can begin your new life as a servant leader.

More Beautiful When Repaired

Are you afraid that as a leader you are damaged goods? Do you believe you have such strong habits of thinking, speaking, and behaving that you could never change? Do you fear you are worse than Humpy Dumpty—that no leadership idea and no coach will ever be able to put you together as a servant leader?

Some of us have known the terrible pain, including headaches, backaches, sleeplessness, and general grumpiness, of being trapped in leadership systems that create an awful choice: follow bad leaders or find something else to do, which could put your career in jeopardy! Are we too far gone? Is it too late?

I want to give you a vision of a preferable future; a vision based in *kintsugi*, the Japanese art of repairing broken ceramics. This art form sweeps up the shattered pieces of what was once a potter's creation. Laying the bits on a table and arranging them in their original form, expert artists use gold powder mixed in a lacquer resin to put the bowl, cup, or plate back together. The resin acts as glue, welding the broken bits of ceramic back together. It leaves a golden band around each former fragment.

A damaged ceramic bowl fixed by *kintsugi* is gorgeous and often more precious and cherished than before it was fractured. People see it as a creative addition to or rebirth of the cup or plate. When it is repaired, it becomes more beautiful in the eye of the owner because of the damage that gives it a history.

I hope that the vision of millions of leaders, in every aspect of human work, being put back together in beautiful ways, will encourage you to become a servant leader and strive for change in the workplace. The next leadership revolution may come from some of us *kintsugi* leaders who say, "Enough of soul-destroying systems of work!"

I encourage you to pay attention to, honor and follow any impulse you have to be a part of the servant leadership movement. Commit your life to leading for the sake of others, not just to the bottom line. Be an evangelist who calls others to consider the merits of servant leadership. I'm asking you to make the choice to be different. To stop right now and reflect on your career. Ask yourself if there is a better way to lead people.

If you say yes, you are signing on for quite a project. And every project needs a project manager. With that in mind I want to pass on to you a life-shaping insight given to me by a mentor: Our projects (e.g., businesses, churches, nonprofits, and service providers) are rarely God's project. *We* are God's project. This is good news for those of us pursuing the transformation of our deepest selves in order to become servant leaders.

Businesses, institutions, and similar entities will come and go. But you, as a person created in God's image, are going to last forever. Let the knowledge of eternal life pull you into becoming the kind of transformed person who, by the grace and power of God, leads for the sake of serving others—in this life and in the life to come.

Next Steps for Servant Leaders

Think about it (reflection). Anyone can test what I've written in this chapter. Simply take Jesus's teaching in the most straightforward manner you can. Get help understanding these teachings if you need it, but you don't have to be a theologian or a biblical scholar to get started trying to love your neighbors, which in this case are your workmates.

Try it (action/application). Note how and when you fail. Think about it. See if any other religious teachings compare favorably to Jesus's. Can you find anything more insightful, more powerful or more transformative? If you can, follow that teaching. If not, intellectual honesty—and probably the call and leading of God—will pull you forward as a follower of Jesus. If you are comfortable doing so, think deeply and pray about your ongoing experience with and wonderment about Jesus. Talk to wise people you trust about what occurs in your heart when you fail. Then begin to work little by little on those heart issues.

Evaluate the results (assessment). Every enterprise needs leadership. Effective servant leadership is the goal of this book.

Looking back over the many new attitudes and practices you have begun to employ, what one personal story would you tell someone to convince him or her of the power, goodness, and business effectiveness of servant leadership?

Conclusion
Servant Leadership: Our Lives Depend on It

What will I experience if I become a servant leader through the apprenticeship of Jesus? I want to leave you with one last bit of wisdom from Jesus—the Servant Leader. I've added, in brackets, a few thoughts to tie it in to this book.

Here's what you can count on:

"Thank you, Father, Lord of heaven and earth. You've concealed your ways from sophisticates and know-it-alls [those committed to old leadership models based on grabbing and using power], but spelled them out clearly to ordinary people [those humble ones willing to venture on servant leadership]. Yes, Father, that's the way you like to work. . . .

"The Father has given me all these things to do and say [the servant leadership I modeled in my life and perfected in my for-others death]. This is a unique Father-Son operation, coming out of Father and Son intimacies and knowledge. No one knows the Son the way the Father does, nor the Father the way the Son does. But I'm not keeping it to myself; I'm ready to go over it line by line with anyone willing to listen, [anyone willing to cultivate the inner reality that energizes and animates servant leaders].

"Are you tired? Worn out? Burned out on religion [on the work cultures created by power, greed, disordered desires]? Come to me. Get away with me and you'll recover your life, [the effective and ethical leader you once dreamed of being]. I'll show you how to take a real rest [by discovering the peace and centeredness there is in servant leadership]. Walk with me and work with me—watch how I do it. Learn the unforced [nonpower-based] rhythms of grace. I won't lay anything heavy or ill-fitting on you. Keep company with me and you'll learn to live [and lead] freely and lightly." (Matthew 11:25-30 *The Message*)

The perspective from which Jesus taught stretches from creation outward to the whole cosmos and encompasses all of human history. From that vantage point, he tells us we don't need to be anxious about anything. There is a divine life, a rule and reign, available to us that is the true home of the human soul. We can enter this realm—the heart of God—by simply placing our confidence in him, becoming his friend and following him. In doing so we can be renewed from the depths of our souls, becoming the kind of leader we would like to follow: one who gets the right stuff done, but does so in the most humane way possible.

From deepest level of motivation and understanding you can muster, make a decision to place your whole confidence and trust in Jesus, and to follow him into the reality of the kingdom of God. Let that reality marinate your inner life— heart, soul, will, and mind—such that when the overflow of your heart is on display at work, those you lead will be nourished by the goodness, strength, and effectiveness of your leadership.

I don't believe it is overstating the matter to say that your career, your whole life, the future of the workplace and thus the character of the human community depends in part on your answer.

Will you do it? Will you place your trust in Jesus? Will you rely on him and follow him? Will you bet your life on Jesus and God's kingdom? Will you become his apprentice in kingdom living—in servant leadership?[1]

Acknowledgments

My first and biggest thanks go to Art and Lori Barter. Their vision for The Servant Leadership Institute to expand from the marketplace to churches and religious non-profits is the soil from which this book grew. They have supported me through thick and thin times and it is my joy to help their vision come to pass. As always I am grateful for the patience and encouragement of my family: my wife, Debbie, and our children, Jonathan and Carol. They make my work possible and are the people who most motivate my work. Holy Trinity Anglican Church in Costa Mesa, California where I am senior pastor, and Churches for the Sake of Others, the diocese of which I am bishop, also get included in this thanksgiving in that they are the main places in which I presently seek to grow as a servant leader. Tony Baron, my friend and colleague, was instrumental in introducing me both to the Anglican world and to the literature of servant leadership. Every author says it, but it is true: this book would not be anywhere close to what it is without the editorial help of my new friend, Cindy Crosby. It was also a delight to reconnect with Cindy Bunch. The additions she suggested transformed the book. I am grateful to the work of the publishing team at Wheatmark for taking this project on. Finally, thanks go to Carol Malinski and Robin Swift at the Servant Leadership Institute. They brought the book across the finish line!

Appendix 1
Young Workers in a Postmodern World

S ervant leadership, based upon my observations and reading, is a suitable fit for the generation now coming into the workforce. Servant leadership creates a work culture in which the most cherished values of younger leaders are best met. These workers, it is often said, are marked by postmodern attitudes. They are often disenchanted with the supposed progress of science and technology. Observing the complex problems of humanity getting worse, these young workers are often suspicious about the capability of human beings to know anything with certainty. This is not a knock on them. They've got as much to offer the workforce as any given generation.

While there is a good match between servant leadership and the eighteen- to thirty-year-old workforce, within that twelve-year span there are subtleties of attitudes and behaviors. I encourage you to check out the literature on this subject. You may want to start with: *Managing the Millennials: Discover the Core Competencies for Managing Today's Workforce* by Chip Espinoza, Mick Ukleja and Craig Rusch; *Not*

Everyone Gets a Trophy: How to Manage Generation Y by Bruce Tulgan; and *Y in the Workplace: Managing the "Me First" Generation* by Nicole A. Lipkin and April J. Perrymore.

Here are ten specific ways I see servant leadership working well for young leaders. Note: these are more-or-less descriptors; they are not meant to bash modernity or faddishly embrace postmodernity.

1. *In postmodernity, truth is found in community, dialogue, context, and perspective, not just scientific rationalism or authoritarian power.* Servant leadership, with its emphasis on relationships and listening, matches up well with this impulse. Listening is not weakness but an act of love, generosity, and hospitality. It brings more truth to the table, more reality to bear and thus more potential for good decision making.

2. *In postmodernity, everyone is accepted or at least tolerated, prejudice is resisted and pluralism is celebrated.* Servant leadership, at its core, demonstrates care for others as individuals and as members of teams. They are not seen as human assets leveraged against metrics or bottom lines. When acceptance is the measure, servant leadership shines.

3. *Postmodernity is marked by an increased sense of justice for all.* Servant leadership, of all models of leadership, meets and exceeds the younger generation's demand for justice.

4. *Postmodernity is often marked by cynicism, skepticism, and a lack of trust in those who have power or are in authority.* The consistent, altruistic behavior—love, respect, and generosity—advocated by servant leadership are the best practices to employ while leading a distrustful work force.

5. *Postmodernity is seen in the discouraged, despairing, and pessimistic mood often associated with young people in the workforce.* Similar to point four, servant leadership has the greatest potential to work with and heal these attitudes.

6. *Postmodernity allows room for many different people to express their gifts of creativity and leadership.* A corporate culture shaped by servant leadership is naturally inclusive and works to discover and cultivate the gifts of others.

7. *Postmodern people crave relationships and community, especially with their families and close friends, and strive to balance work, family, and friends.* A servant-led corporate culture has the most potential to facilitate this balance.

8. *Postmodern people thrive on creativity and alternate ways of doing things; they are willing to risk new ideas.* Servant leadership is an alternate and creative way of doing things in the workplace.

9. *Postmodernism looks for something that transcends the usual power-based, power-enforced modes of knowledge.* Servant leadership includes wisdom, story, mystery, and spirituality, which offer a new and safe mode of knowledge.

10. *Postmodernism intuitively values mentoring, not command and control systems. Young workers do not normally respect nonrelational power and authority.* Mentoring as practiced by a servant leader gives managers and supervisors a way to connect with the postmodern workforce.

Appendix 2

St. Ignatius of Loyola's
Prayer of Examen

G rowth in any endeavor—and especially concerning the personal growth necessary for servant leadership—happens best in the context of routine, honest, nonjudgmental assessment. This is why at the end of each chapter you were asked to reflect on your progress in and the challenges of servant leadership, to reflect on what is happening in your heart, will, soul, mind, and emotions.

You were also asked to be present to the reactions of those you lead. Body language, facial expressions, and tone of voice are crucial indications of how others experience our presence—our attitudes, words, and actions. Most of us need something to assist us in becoming more aware, more alert to what is real about us and the environment our leadership is creating at work.

I want to introduce you to an ancient form of prayer, the prayer of examen. It was designed to help Jesus-followers grow in their relationship to him. The prayer of examen is designed to help us live and lead in *examined* ways. According to a website on spirituality, "The Daily Examen is a technique of prayerful reflection on the events of the day in order to detect God's presence and discern his direction for us. The Examen is an ancient practice . . . that can help us see God's hand at work in our whole experience."[1]

To get started with the prayer of examen, you will want to practice it once a day for ten to fifteen minutes, perhaps just after work, or after a workout and dinner, or maybe before you go to bed.

Find a comfortable place where you can be still. Then, as a way to examine your inner world and your day, sit for a few moments and read the following prayer:

Search me, God, and know my heart;
> test me and know my anxious thoughts.
> See if there is any offensive way in me,
> and lead me in the way everlasting. (Psalm 139:23-24)

As you sit with the words of the Psalm and reflect on your day, try to make the thoughts and ideas of this prayer your own. Here are three examples:

Search. "I don't know God; I am not sure I trust you or this process. It seems a bit weird and made up." Or maybe you notice the opposite is true: "Oh God, I hate that I lost my patience again today and went off on that woman (or man) at work. Please show me the broken places in my heart where those words and behaviors come from."

God. "God, I am not sure you exist. But this book is full of references to you. Do you exist? If so, can you help me to know your reality so I can both come to grips with and rely on you?" Or maybe the word *God* leads you to begin to thank him for accompanying you along the journey of inner transformation that is essential to servant leadership.

Heart. Maybe the word *heart* reminds you that you are a whole person, not just a body or brain. As you are made mindful of your interior life, you might want to use *heart* as a trigger to begin to talk to God about what you thought, felt, or observed in your leadership today, or how others led you.

Keep turning the psalm into prayer in that manner. There is no right or wrong way to do so. In the beginning, allow yourself to be guided in the process by whatever seems most real, most honest, most genuinely true about you and the people and events of your day. The prayer of examen is strong and has broad shoulders: it can prop the beginner up and embrace the deepest of thinking. Trust it. Trust the process. In a few weeks or months you will find yourself coming to powerful new insights about yourself, your work and the people you interact with.

With the psalm as our usher into examen, we turn next to a few prayer prompts that are intended to walk us though the remaining prayerful examination of our day. The following comes from my friend Larry Warner. Larry is the founder and executive director of *b* (b-ing.org). A lifelong student of Ignatian prayer, and an adjunct professor at Bethel Seminary in San Diego, Larry teaches at Talbot Seminary's Institute for Spiritual Formation and the master's in ministry program at Point Loma Nazarene University.

Prayer Prompts

Silence and gratitude. Become aware of God's presence. You are always and everywhere with God (Acts 17:28). Recall particular good things you've experienced since your last examen (James 1:17).

Search. God knows your heart. Ask God to reveal things in your heart and life that are hurtful to you or others, knowing there is no condemnation in God's love (Psalm 139:23; Romans 8:1).

Review and awareness. Ask: Where have the interactions and circumstances of my life been taking me—away from or to God? When do I notice the love of God? How did I respond to God? What challenged me? When did I say yes to God? In what circumstances did I resist God?

Talk with Jesus. Honestly converse with Jesus about what you notice. Attend to these things in prayer: ask for forgiveness, counsel, and guidance; give thanks; and know that you are loved, accepted, and forgiven in Christ.

Abiding. Acknowledge your need of God's abiding presence to live a God-honoring life as a servant leader (John 15:5). Cultivate an ever-deepening internalization of God's love for you (Ephesians 3:17-19), God's faithfulness to you (Hebrews 13:5), and God's power within you (Ephesians 3:16).

The Lord's Prayer

The following includes a traditional version of the Lord's Prayer and a modern adaptation by Dallas Willard. For your daily practice choose the version that best connects your heart to God. Or use both as you choose on any given day.

> Our Father in heaven,
> hallowed be your name,
> your kingdom come,
> your will be done,
>   on earth as it is in heaven.
> Give us this day our daily bread.

And forgive us our debts,
    as we also have forgiven our debtors.
And lead us not into temptation,
    but deliver us from the evil one.
For yours is the kingdom
    and the power
    and the glory forever and ever. Amen.
    (Matthew 6:9-13)

Dear Father always near us,
May your name be treasured and loved,
May your rule be completed in us—
May your will be done here on earth
In just the way it is done in heaven.
Give us today the things we need today,
And forgive us our sins and impositions on you
As we are forgiving all who in any way offend us.
Please don't put us through trials, but deliver us from
    anything bad.
Because you are the one in charge, and you have all the
    power,
And the glory too is all yours—forever—
Which is just the way we want it!

Appendix 3

Recommended Reading

The following books on spiritual disciplines are designed to get you connected to the grace and power of God for the transformation of your heart. If you follow these authors' bibliographies you will discover many other outstanding books.

Foster, Richard. *Celebration of Discipline*. 3rd ed. San Francisco: HarperSanFrancisco, 2002

Nouwen, Henri. *The Way of the Heart*. New York: HarperCollins, 2009.

Peterson, Eugene. *Practice Resurrection*. Grand Rapids: Eerdmans, 2010.

Smith, James Bryan. *The Good and Beautiful Life*. Downers Grove, IL: IVP Books, 2009.

Willard, Dallas. *The Spirit of the Disciplines*. New York: HarperCollins, 1999.

Endnotes

Introduction

1. "Engaging Employees: What Drives Employee Engagement and Why It Matters," Dale Carnegie Training, www.dalecarnegie.com/imap/white_papers/employee_engagement_white_paper.

2. Max Depree, *Leading Without Power* (San Francisco: Jossey-Bass, 1997), pp. 186-87.

3. See for instance Don Frick, Doug Hoxeng and Jeff Panther, *The Business Case for Servant Leadership: Lessons in Success from Organizations and Leaders* (Phoenix: Ken Blanchard Executive MBA, 2009); James A. Autry, *The Servant Leader: How to Build a Creative Team, Develop Great Morale, and Improve Bottom-Line Performance* (New York: Crown Business, 2004); and Tony Baron, *The Art of Servant Leadership* (Tucson: Wheatmark, 2013.

4. Max De Pree, quoted in A. C. Macris and Lawrence A. Reiter, "Why I Am So Important: The Case for Servant Leadership," *Macris Group Update Newsletter* 8 (October 2010): 4.

5. For additional background on servant leadership, see Robert Greenleaf and Larry C. Spears, *Servant Leadership: A Journey into the Nature of Legitimate Power and Greatness*, 25th anniv. ed. (Mahwah, NJ: Paulist Press, 2002); Max DePree, *Leading Without Power* (San Francisco: Jossey-Bass, 2003); John Maxwell, *The 21 Irrefutable Laws of Leadership* (Nash-

ville: Thomas Nelson, 2007), esp. chaps. 5, 10, 12, 18; Ken Blanchard and Phil Hodges, *The Servant Leader* (Nashville: Thomas Nelson, 2003); Ken Blanchard, *Lead Like Jesus* (Nashville: Thomas Nelson, 2008).

6. Brad Plumer, "The Biggest Question Facing the U.S. Economy: Why Are People Dropping Out of the Workforce?" *Washington Post*, January 10, 2014, www.washingtonpost.com/blogs/wonkblog/wp/2014/01/10/the-biggest-question-facing-the-u-s-economy-why-are-people-dropping-out-of-the-workforce.

7. This nationally known retail store is in almost every mall or retail area in America.

Chapter 1

1. See for instance Robert K. Greenleaf, *Servant Leadership: A Journey into the Nature of Legitimate Power and Greatness,* 25th anniv. ed. (Mahwah, NJ: Paulist Press, 2002).

2. Henry Cloud, *Integrity: The Courage to Meet the Demands of Reality* (New York: HarperBusiness, 2006), p. 143.

3. Kelli B. Grant, "Americans Hate Their Jobs, Even with Office Perks," CNBC.com, June 24, 2013, www.cnbc.com/id/100835261#.

4. Ibid.

Chapter 2

1. Dallas Willard, "*The Craftiness of Christ,*" *Dallas Willard* (blog), www.dwillard.org/articles/artview.asp?artID=101.

2. Madeleine L'Engle, *Walking on Water* (Colorado Springs: WaterBrook, 1972), p. 90.

3. See Jesus's teachings on fruit-bearing trees and cleaning the outside of cups and tombs (Matthew 7:18; 12:33; 23:25-27).

4. T. S. Eliot, *Four Quartets* (New York: Harcourt, 1943), p. 14.

Chapter 3

1. *Dallas Willard, The Divine Conspiracy* (New York: Harper, 1998), pp. 93-95.

2. I am indebted to Dallas Willard for this idea. For his complete

thoughts please see *The Spirit of the Disciplines* (San Francisco: HarperCollins, 1991), pp. 7-9.

3. I am indebted to Dallas Willard for these two thoughts. I, along with many other colleagues of Willard, heard Dallas say them many times when we taught or worked together in various settings.
4. Ken Blanchard and Phil Hodges, *Lead Like Jesus* (Nashville: Thomas Nelson, 2006), p. 39.
5. T. S. Eliot, *Four Quartets* (New York: Harcourt, 1943), pp. 45, 32.
6. Ibid., p. 44.

Chapter 4

1. Dallas Willard, "Willard Words," *Dallas Willard* (blog), www.dwillard.org/resources/WillardWords.asp.
2. *The Karate Kid*, directed by John G. Avildsen (1984; Culver City, CA: Columbia Pictures).

Chapter 5

1. Bob Dylan, "Gotta Serve Somebody," *Slow Train Coming*, Columbia Records, 1979.
2. David G. Benner, *Surrender to Love* (Downers Grove, IL: Inter-Varsity Press, 2003), pp. 41-41.
3. Ibid., p. 76.
4. Ibid., p. 93.
5. Ibid.
6. Henry Cloud, *Integrity: The Courage to Meet the Demands of Reality* (New York: HarperBusiness, 2006), p. 8.
7. Ibid., p. 24.
8. Ibid., p. 106.
9. Ibid., p. 107.
10. Ibid., p. 282.
11. Edwin Friedman, *A Failure of Nerve* (New York: Seabury, 2007), pp. 183, 14.

Chapter 6

1. I am indebted to Max De Pree for this idea, but I can't find it as a direct quote in any of his books. However, I recommend three of his books: *Leadership Is an Art*, *Leadership Jazz* and most important for servant leaders *Leading Without Power*.
2. Madeleine L'Engle, *Walking on Water* (Colorado Springs: WaterBrook, 1972), p. 128.

Chapter 7

1. Parker Palmer, *Let Your Life Speak* (San Francisco: Jossey-Bass, 2000), p. 64.
2. Max De Pree, *Leadership Is an Art* (New York: Dell, 2004), p. 9.
3. C. S. Lewis, *The Weight of Glory and Other Addresses* (Grand Rapids: Eerdmans, 1949), p. 15.
4. Walter C. Wright Jr., "The Legacy of Max De Pree," *Cardus*, March 1, 2002, www.cardus.ca/comment/article/1297/the-legacy-of-max-de-pree.
5. Max DePree, *Leadership Is an Art* (New York: Bantam Double-day, 1989), pp. 9-10.
6. For De Pree's full ideas see the chapters "The Millwright Died" and "Intimacy" in ibid.
7. Ibid.
8. Ibid.

Chapter 8

1. Robert Greenleaf, "Ten Principles of Servant Leadership," Butler University, www.butler.edu/volunteer/resources/princi-ples-of-servant-leadership.
2. Tom Wright, *Lent for Everyone: Mark, Year B* (Louisville: West-minster John Know, 2012), p. 142.
3. Ken Blanchard and Phil Hodges, *Lead Like Jesus* (Nashville: Thomas Nelson, 2006), p. 84.
4. Dallas Willard, quoted by David Steinhart, "Dallas Willard on

Humility," *Crosswalk.com*, www.crosswalk.com/blogs/dr-ray-pritchard/dallas-willard-on-humility-1330252.html.

Chapter 9

1. Elaine Scarry, *On Beauty* (Princeton, NJ: Princeton University Press, 1999), pp. 118, 115, 88.
2. Madeleine L'Engle, *Walking on Water* (Wheaton, IL: Harold Shaw, 1980), pp. 9-10.
3. Ibid., p. 65.
4. Ibid., p. 89.
5. Elaine Scarry, *On Beauty and Being Just* (Princeton, NJ: Princeton University Press, 1999), p. 30.

Conclusion

1. For a more complete picture of the eternal and spiritual nature of human beings, I recommend two books by C. S. Lewis: *The Weight of Glory and Other Addresses* (Grand Rapids: Eerdmans, 1949), and *The Great Divorce* (New York: Macmillan, 1946).

Appendix 2

1. "The Daily Examen," *Ignatian Spirituality*, www.ignatianspirituality.com/ignatian-prayer/the-examen.

Other titles by
Todd Hunter

Christianity Beyond Belief
Giving Church Another Chance
The Accidental Anglican
Our Favorite Sins

About the Author

Todd Hunter is the founding bishop of The Diocese of Churches for the Sake of Others and the founding pastor of Holy Trinity Anglican Church in Costa Mesa, CA. He is past President of Alpha USA and former National Director for the Association of Vineyard Churches.

He is author of *Christianity Beyond Belief, Giving Church Another Chance, The Outsider Interviews, The Accidental Anglican,* and *Our Favorite Sins.*

Todd has been an adjunct professor of evangelism, leadership in contemporary culture, and spiritual formation at George Fox University, Fuller Seminary, Western Seminary, Vanguard University, Azusa Pacific University, Biblical Seminary, and Wheaton College. In addition, he has been a Distinguished Lecturer at several institutions of higher learning.

Todd has written articles for study Bibles, dictionaries, and encyclopedias as well as key publications such as *Christianity Today, Charisma, Outreach,* and *Ministries Today.*

About Servant Leadership Institute

There is a need in the world for a new kind of leader, one who serves versus rules over those who follow. Traditional control-based management creates a pressure cooker that destroys employee initiative, eliminates trust, lowers efficiency, and increases costs. In a world where employee engagement is a major concern, we believe servant leadership is more than just a solution to a problem; it's a better way to lead.

The Servant Leadership Institute (SLI) exists to inspire and equip leaders to lead in a different way. Servant leaders foster an environment of trust and respect at all levels in an organization. At SLI, we are passionate about helping people find meaning and purpose in their work as they achieve success through servant leadership.

As implementers, we offer a refreshing "others first" mindset in the leadership development space. We provide:

» Consulting, training and coaching (CTC).

» Thought-provoking conferences and workshops that inspire a mindset of serving.

» Content that supports building and maintaining a servant-led culture.

To learn more, visit www.servantleadershipinstitute.com or call us at 855-754-5323.

CPSIA information can be obtained at www.ICGtesting.com
Printed in the USA
BVOW02s0144110216

436295BV00001B/9/P